"Sarah's honest and insightful work is the fruit of her courage, imagination, and hard-won wisdom. Sarah prayerfully and poetically sketches the sacred terrain of vocation, risk, imagination, struggle, stillness, and growth. Her reflections will draw you into a longing for greater wholeness and embodiment in your own life—to play, to tell, and be."

—Jesse Size
Author of *Dust and Ashes*

"Pastors face impossible expectations: create innovative ministries (but not too innovative), maintain our sacred traditions (but don't be too churchy), and pour yourself out for others (but schedule some self-care!). In *Play. Tell. Be.*, Sarah Agnew offers a new way for clergy and lay leaders, one that enables us to be our truest selves while engaging the joys and challenges of ministry. It is life-giving. It is necessary. It is liberating."

—Jo Schonewolf
Cohost of *What the Hell is a Pastor*

"Sarah Agnew leads us through *Pray. Tell. Be.* with ease and wit, her graceful prose matched only by a poetry as raw as it is rhythmic. Using her own stories as entry points, this brilliant storyteller-poet-minister offers a grounded hope in ways even more meaningful because she's lived them. Sarah is the real deal—a twenty-first-century bard—and this book, with its opportunities for reflection, rest, and renewal, is a real gift."

—Jason Chesnut
Pastor, Anam Cara Community

"This is a very honest account of Sarah's life and her ministry. She charts her movement away from church and then back into its center. Underneath these events she grapples with the challenges she faces from her health issues and her own wellbeing. For anyone involved in church leadership you will find rest and renewal for your soul in reading this and learning from Sarah's journey."

—Dave Male
Visiting Lecturer, Luther Seminary, Minneapolis

"In contrast to how we are often driven to think about successful outcomes, Sarah uses thoughtful and thought-provoking self-reflection to consider how she teaches and learns, gives and receives, follows and leads. She invites us to consider our connections to her stories and provides prompts to creatively consider what has passed and what is emerging."

—**Ruth Sims**
Organizational Development and Communications Professional

Play. Tell. Be.

Play. Tell. Be.

Postures for Leading and Living Well

SARAH AGNEW

RESOURCE *Publications* • Eugene, Oregon

PLAY. TELL. BE.
Postures for Leading and Living Well

Copyright © 2025 Sarah Agnew. All rights reserved. Except for brief quotations in critical publications or reviews, no part of this book may be reproduced in any manner without prior written permission from the publisher. Write: Permissions, Wipf and Stock Publishers, 199 W. 8th Ave., Suite 3, Eugene, OR 97401.

Resource Publications
An Imprint of Wipf and Stock Publishers
199 W. 8th Ave., Suite 3
Eugene, OR 97401

www.wipfandstock.com

PAPERBACK ISBN: 979-8-3852-5424-8
HARDCOVER ISBN: 979-8-3852-5425-5
EBOOK ISBN: 979-8-3852-5426-2

VERSION NUMBER 082525

Scripture quotations are from New Revised Standard Version Bible: Anglicized Edition, copyright © 1989, 1995 National Council of the Churches of Christ in the United States of America. Used by permission. All rights reserved worldwide.

Scripture quotations marked (CEB) are from the COMMON ENGLISH BIBLE. © Copyright 2011 COMMON ENGLISH BIBLE. All rights reserved. Used by permission. (www.CommonEnglishBible.com).

The poem "Off the Edge" appeared previously in *Seasons of the Heart*, edited by Jude Aquilina, John Pfitzner, and Russell Talbot (Adelaide: Effective Living Centre, 2010) and is republished with permission.

The poems "On the Healing Nature of Green" and "With" appeared previously in *Whisper on My Palm* by Sarah Agnew (Eugene, OR: Resource, 2022) and are republished with permission from the publisher.

The poem "Of the Instant Goodbyes" appeared previously in *From the Mist* by Sarah Agnew (Eugene, OR: Resource, 2025) and is republished with permission from the publisher.

For those who invite me to accompany you.
For those who accompany me.
We are only fully human, together.

Contents

Acknowledgments | ix
Prelude | xi
Introduction | xvii

Part One: Play
Leaving and returning | 3
Playing on the Edge | 15
Growth rather than "outcomes" | 36
Play: embodied and costly | 43

Part Two: Tell
Story | 57
Discerning | 60
Storyteller | 63
Poet | 71
Minister | 76
Discovery: identity and vocation | 82
Scholar | 90

Part Three: Be
A Ministry of Presence | 101
Sacred Presence | 111
Chronically Fatigued | 119
A contemplative way of being | 130

Postlude: Not to lead, but to accompany each other
Mutuality | 151
Learning to accompany and live well | 154
Play. Tell. Be. A Rule of Sacred Presence. | 156

Appendix: Wellbeing resources | 157

Bibliography | 159

Acknowledgments

THIS BOOK DRAWS FROM a lifetime of experiences, of participating in community: there are of course many, many people who have shared those experiences, shaped those communities, with me. To try to name any individually might be to court gross errors of omission.

So, reader, if you find yourself in these pages, between the lines, behind the scenes: thank you for your part in my story, and for my part in yours.

I have gleaned wisdom from, and been supported, equipped, and encouraged by numerous mentors, teachers, guides. Some are named within these pages, some hinted at; all deeply appreciated, your presence gifts I treasure and examples I hope to emulate.

Family of birth, chosen family, close friends, you are here, with me, also and always. Cheering, teaching, tending wounds, loving and inviting me to offer the same for you. Thank you.

Prelude

I woke on a Monday morning feeling low, out of sorts, tired, achy. Were these symptoms of the ME/Chronic Fatigue[1] or Depression with which I live, or a reaction to stress? Or perhaps all of the above? Monday is my day off, my non-negotiable day off; a day for solitude, stillness, and silence that allows me to give my all on Sunday when I facilitate the weekly gathering of my congregation for their work of worship. The day opened before me with space to feel the blues and let them be.

I played the stupid game on my phone for an hour. But it neither helps the body aches, nor my mood. The game is a means by which I hide, from my thoughts, emotions, the world. I know it, and I find it difficult to quit the habit.

Eventually, I got up—hunger the impetus. Still in my pajamas, I had breakfast, then moved to the dining table and the 1000-piece jigsaw puzzle I had started the day before.

At some point, hours later, hunger again eventually led me to check the fridge, but I couldn't decide on anything I had that I wanted to eat, so knowing the Diabetes needs me to have food somewhat regularly, I ordered pizza, and watched the next *Murdoch Mysteries* DVD while I ate.

I did turn off the TV and return to the puzzle, enacting my choice for quiet on Mondays. Then watched a few more episodes over dinner.

After dinner, puzzle now complete, I read, finishing the book in which I'd been engrossed for several days: *Surprised by God*, by Rabbi Danya Ruttenberg. Choosing silence still, I then picked up the coloring book and felt pens I keep beside the armchair, rather than the remote control. That felt good, but I still felt—meh.

---

1. Myalgic Encephalomyalitis, which is commonly known as Chronic Fatigue Syndrome. In fact, chronic fatigue is the major symptom of ME, which is chronic muscle pain (Myalgia) and swelling in the brain and spinal cord (encephalomyelitis), causing dysregulation of energy production at a cellular level. ME/CFS features throughout this book; I will tell the story of my experience with this illness in Part Three: Be. I have included a list of resources for learning more about ME/CFS in Appendix A.

PRELUDE

At some stage in the afternoon between TV and puzzle, I had enacted breathing and tapping practices I had learned,[2] and sought to listen to the angst, the sad. I'm not sure I found the words then, but I felt the feelings: I paid attention, I saw my self and knew I was seen. And it helped.

I tried not to play the game on the phone before sleep; I had done so well not accessing screens for those hours before going to bed, and the jazz was relaxing and bringing me joy as I listened.

But, inevitably, I reached for my phone.

I had heard from Dan Plonk at the minister's day last week that I was probably diminishing the quality of the sleep I desperately needed; but the game exhausted the thoughts and made my eyes tired enough to close.

The morning after began in the same way. I tried to lie there listening to the chants of Hildegard of Bingen—but the habit, the phone, the game, the hiding from the world I did not want to enter . . .

And then, after an hour, something suddenly seemed to click within.

The previous week, I had been talking with a friend who had begun a morning practice of watching ABC Breakfast. I lamented with her my sense of disconnection from the world and current events, suspecting it was a missing element in my weekly reflections with the congregation. My friend told me what I would have suspected: ABC Breakfast is serious news with the lightness of stories of life well lived. Good company. Informed awareness of the world. Perhaps it might work for me, I thought.

But I don't drink herbal tea, and I do want to delay the first coffee of the day. A stumbling block for some reason—why I couldn't decide simply to get up and watch the breakfast program?!

This Tuesday morning, however, it occurred to me that I might like to drink a big glass of water first thing. That I could savor that, as I connected with the world. And it got me out of bed with the joy of anticipation. Joy that continued as I appreciated hearing of situations unfolding in the world, of Indigenous hip hop and autistic journalism students, and witnessed the warmth between colleagues in the final week for one on this show she had anchored for five years.

As I reflected with my supervisor later that morning, I rambled over lots of things in quick succession as usual, and arrived at some insights.

---

2. Breathing work guided over the years by practitioners of Network Spinal Chiropractic Treatment. Tapping is a feature of EFT counselling. Again, resources in Appendix A.

PRELUDE

The "meh" feeling of the day before held a couple of things within it. First, "meh" held some anger and feeling uncared for by the Church, as I sought redress, sought to be seen, and heard, and received none of it. Second, "meh" seemed also to hold the discomfort of wrestling with ideas, challenges, and invitations that came as I read Danya Ruttenberg's story of spiritual awakening. I seem to have felt that my responses and choices ought to be to do as this author had done. Danya Ruttenberg had found herself drawn to fairly rigorous disciplined following of Jewish religious practices; I felt my own religious practice, my discipline, wanting in comparison. Ruttenberg says in her book, as I do in this one, for that matter: do not compare yourself to me or anyone else. Listen, observe, learn, and find the practices that are life-giving for *you*.

As I reflected on my choices through the "meh" of the previous day, I noticed that I had actually enacted my own practices that I had been developing over the years. In *my* way, I acted with discipline.

- I paid attention and got curious about how I was feeling
- I chose to be still and silent even as I was tempted to drown out emotion with noise
- I chose play
- I chose to listen
- Yes, I withdrew, *and* I am making my withdrawal a retreat *into* self and Sacred presence, rather than *away from* the world
- I found my way to enact the next new element of my practice—(re)connecting with and paying attention to the world.

My supervisor gave me the phrase "that's weird" as the response we might offer, when we realize we have again picked up baggage we seek to let go. As a response to many of life's challenges and hurdles, our choices we thought we did not want to make. "That's weird," as in I am curious, let me look at that further and seek to understand. Not, that's hard or difficult, let me look away and hold it at a distance.

that's weird

Moving is tough work today,

PRELUDE

my body aches, my back
is breaking, my arms weighed
down by something heavy—oh,
that's weird, the suitcase I had
thought safely tucked in place is in my
hands again. I wonder why that is?

And what was I doing
with this baggage? I remember,
stowing it away—I lift
it up and turn to fit and as
I do it opens—that's weird:
I wonder what that is, hanging out?

I put down the case, pull
at the threads and sit,
take time to look, to see;
to rub the scars this bow
had left on me, this arrow
and others, too—and to notice
these wounds no longer throb
with constancy, but do itch
a little, occasionally.

I tuck the bow back into its story,
shut the case and stand
to lift it, somehow lighter
than it was mere moments ago—
that's weird; I wonder
if those arrows fell away
as I put the bow in place?

Then I slide the case
into its slot, and moving
with more ease, the aches
and pains released for now, I
turn and give the bag a pat—
that's weird, I note, I used to hate
that baggage.

Curiosity. Diving deeper. Paying attention.

Prelude

Play. Tell. Be.

Welcome to my reflections on how I have come to learn and adopt these postures that help me to lead, and live, with deeper wellness every day. May my story encourage you in your own.

Introduction

> The contemplative's intention and focused attention during contemplation is graced by the generosity of God who desires to share a glimpse of Their Holy self with us. All that is needed is to consent to God's invitation for communion in silence and solitude.
>
> Rolf Nolasco, *The Contemplative Counselor*

Learning to be present

IN RESPONSE TO LIFE'S circumstances, my unfolding identity and calling, and the choice of others to "follow" me, I have been experimenting with postures that help me to be more present—with others, with my self, with creation, with the Holy. This book is not merely another on "leadership", although it may provide an alternative set of postures to more dominant approaches to leadership that are celebrated. I don't know about you, but the business model, CEO type, and growth and money focus to leadership, within many parts of the church and community organizations, does not resonate well with me. This book is not exactly a memoir, although it does contain my rememberings of seasons and experiences, of growing and becoming. This is certainly *not* a how-to guide on wellbeing, mindfulness, or leadership. As usual, I find myself transgressing boundaries, crossing genres, doing things my own way—may that be your story too. This book is, I hope, a conversation, an instigator of conversation "with" you, as you hear my story and reflect on your own. *Play. Tell. Be. Postures for Leading and Living Well* is a book offering my reflections on becoming, on the journey I have walked so far in becoming the creative woman of God I have always felt drawn towards being. I hope it might encourage you in your becoming.

Introduction

Who am I? I introduce myself as a storyteller-poet-minister. I identify most with my Scottish heritage, and there is English and Norwegian via New Zealand in my ancestry also. I was born and raised on Kaurna Land, Adelaide, in South Australia; live here again after seven years away in Edinburgh, Scotland, and the Australian Capital of Canberra on Ngunnawal/Ngambri Land. I grew up in the Uniting Church in Australia, which formed from Congregational, Methodist, and Presbyterian churches in 1977. Everything else you need to know, you will discover as this story unfolds, or can find at sarahagnew.com.au.

If, as my friend Ruth Sims suggests, leaders are made by their followers,[3] I began this project of reflecting on how I am a leader by considering what others may have seen in me that they would choose to follow me.

I am prepared to take risks, to play, explore, experiment, and have confidence enough to "fail."

I understand story and storytelling. I am someone who is trusted to tell and hear, to hold and facilitate, our stories as a community and as individuals, storytelling a practice leading us towards healing and wholeness.

I have always been present, attentive, to the Sacred, and had a natural empathy with others. We sense such characteristics in others, don't we? We will gravitate towards those with such a posture, for safety, encouragement, guidance.

I have not chosen to be a "leader."

I have discerned something in my being that aligns with the role of ordained Minister of the Word and Sacraments in my tradition, the Uniting Church in Australia (UCA). My church has discerned this with me.

I have not chosen to *be* a leader.

I have chosen to find a way of living into my being as a *creative woman of God*. I remember naming it thus, when I turned from the path of English Literature academic. I had been accepted for a PhD but not for a scholarship, making a move to Perth, Western Australia too difficult. I found I was not committed enough, not passionate enough for that particular risk. On reflection, I found this path did not feel as though it would lead me into being *a creative woman of God*. I wanted to be more deeply embedded in faithful community. Mum might be right: if the UCA had a monastic order, at that point I may have chosen to enter the religious life. In some ways I have, anyway. The vocation that unfolded through the years of discernment

---

3. https://www.ruth-sims.com

Introduction

has within it a call to an "order", a call to singleness, and if not a call to, then certainly a consequence of some level of "poverty". Over the years, I have felt an ever-deepening call into a contemplative, or monastic way of living; I name my home my "Wee Hermitage," and understand my role in faithful community to be a "Ministry of Presence." So that now, I seem to have further defined my sense of being as *a creative, contemplative, woman of Holy One*.

I find that with this ever-evolving understanding of my becoming, I want to understand how I have grown to this point. To reflect on the qualities of my character and living that seem attractive to others. To reflect on my choices in response to others gathering around me, inviting me to be present with them in community.

Postures for leading and being: Play, Tell, Be.

As I reflected, I found I have developed three overarching postures in my being. These postures form the structure for the book, roughly chronological in its overall narrative, while weaving back and forward a bit as we go. As an artist, a poet and performer, my creativity, imagination, intuition—my capacity to *play*—attracts others to join me. As a Minister in the Uniting Church and a storyteller, I tell the story of Christian spirituality, the stories held in the Bible, and I tell and help others *tell* our stories: story invites others to join me. As a holder of story, a poet, a contemplative, and as a person living with chronic illness, I have practiced discipline, enacted rhythm, gradually learned to simply, profoundly, *be* present—with myself, with others, with the Sacred. My capacity to *be* draws others into their own *being*.

I wrote this book as an exercise in reflection for myself. Reflecting on what I have learned through experience in community, in the search for wellbeing; as I learn to live well with others choosing to follow me, learn to live well with chronic illness. Douglas Purnell considers a tendency towards too much "privacy among spiritual leaders about their life and being" to be neither "helpful or fitting."[4] Part of our role is to be open; to foster a healthy enough self-understanding to participate in the mutual vulnerability of life in community that allows us to share of ourselves openly and honestly; and in sharing our stories, strengthen ourselves, each other, and our community. The ten-year anniversary of my ordination as a Minister of the Word

---

4. Douglas Purnell, *Being in Ministry. Honestly, Openly, and Deeply*. Eugene, OR: Wipf & Stock, 2010, 10.

Introduction

in the Uniting Church seemed a spark for such reflection. Several years later, it is written, and I wonder if my story might hold encouragement for you in the living of your story.

I offer you my story for the reason I tell any story, the reason all of us humans tell stories. We tell stories because we are fully human together, and we are strengthened as individuals and communities in the sharing of our stories. Indeed, we each have a *responsibility* to tell our story to encourage others, to hear others' stories to nurture wellbeing for us all.[5]

A rough guide

As I mentioned, this is not *quite* a chronological narrative. I group stories around the postures of play, story, and presence. A rough guide might help orient you as we set out.

We are heading back towards that Monday of presence with the "meh"; that Tuesday of discovery. To how I am living and "leading" today, how I got here, and why I choose this way of being. We are heading towards a rule or way of life that holds me well enough through chronic illness; that caught me when I fell in a time of trauma and brokenness; and that helps me to thrive and facilitate meaningful encounters for others that nurture their thriving in life and community.

I call it a Rule of Sacred Presence. It emerges out of playfulness, experimentation, trial and error and trying again. It is grounded in storytelling and the Sacred Story my community of faith, those of Christian Spirituality, enact. It is a set of seven practices or postures that encourage me to be where I am and pay attention. We will get to this Rule of Sacred Presence through Play, Storytelling, and a Ministry of Presence.

In "Play", we start with me leaving the church, and through art, creativity, and experimentation, finding my way back into vibrant communities of faith. I find my way back even to the point of so aligning myself with the church as to join its order of clergy, set apart within the whole to help us gather and remember the story we live as people on the Way of Love.

I experimented with jazz church and story church. I played with the process of formation for ordination by starting a new church experiment as

---

5. Daniel Taylor, *Creating a Spiritual Legacy: How to Share Your Stories, Values, and Wisdom.* United States: Baker Publishing Group, 2011.

Introduction

part of my training. I failed. Jazz church and story church had shorter lives than we would have liked. I planted seeds. The vocation of storyteller-poet-minister was forged in these experiments, these sandpits of play.

In "Play", then, we start outside church and find our way back through creativity, imagination, and the courage and willingness to "fail."

In "Tell", we retrace some steps from Part One, as I take another look at the discernment that led to hearing a call to ordained ministry. Preaching, learning biblical languages, and identifying the storyteller within are steps we take through "Tell". We meet the Network of Biblical Storytellers, and learn something about my scholarship *as* a biblical storyteller. As I grew into this call to ordained ministry, I discerned its broader context within a vocation and identity as storyteller-poet-minister, so I will share with you something of each of these facets, and how they come together. In "Tell", we weave back and forth through time a bit, consider symbol and sign and story, through the act of telling itself.

"Be" will weave threads together as I describe the emerging and shaping of my Rule of Sacred Presence. Creation. Mutuality. Learning to live with ME/Chronic Fatigue Syndrome, building on learning from living well with Depression. Vulnerability and the strength that takes. Paying attention and learning to trust what we have learnt and who we are becoming. Listening to the Holy, to self, to each other. In "Be", we go deeper again into vulnerability, and consider one way to shape a rule of life with authenticity, for living, for "leading"—or accompanying each other—well.

At pivotal moments in my life, cross-roads and turning points, I have chosen a direction that feels as though it will take me towards my becoming as a *creative woman of God*. I am not giving you my entire biography. I am certainly not giving you a how-to guide. I share with you some stories of my living, as I learn to step outside of the world's loud noises about who we're "supposed" to be.

I will tell you about choosing singleness.

I will tell you about living with a Black Dog and ME/Chronic Fatigue.

I will invite you to pause, rest, listen and ponder; to bring your story into conversation with mine, as we seek authentic ways to live, to be, well, together.

Part One: Play

> Play is the most perfect expression of the life of one completely reliant upon the grace of God. In playing there is no thought of the production of any "thing" for the common good, no sense of the need to "do something" that will justify one's existence.
>
> Brian Edgar, *The God Who Plays*

Leaving and returning

I left the church

NOT HOW YOU EXPECTED the reflections from a "leader" in the church to begin, I imagine. It wasn't for long, in the end. But I did decide not to attend worship with my family any more. I had a job in a bookshop in the city. I was offered work on Sundays. I said yes. For all my life until that moment I would have said no, even with the higher pay rate. As a teenager I said no to joining a swim squad when practice was held on Friday nights. Youth group met on Friday nights, and that was my priority, at 12 years of age. I joined leadership teams at youth group, that junior iteration, and later the senior one. My commitment was a quality others saw in me and valued; the capacity to lead, too, although I took longer to identify and articulate both for myself.

I had been in leadership roles for almost ten years, a member for all of my 21, when I stopped attending church. I had been leading within *this* congregation, the second community of faith I had known, for two or three. I played clarinet in the band for leading worship. I had been on Church Council, and volunteered in the office, which gave me experience that helped me get my first proper paid job. And I left the church.

Here are some of the reasons I left.

Ageism

On Church Council, I had been the "youth" member. At the time, congregations were encouraged to designate places on councils and committees especially for younger folk, to help us to be involved, contribute, break through the gates held closed by older generations. Some of the "proper" members did not treat *me* as such. They figuratively patted me on the head when I spoke, then ignored or appropriated as their own, my ideas,

Part One: Play

insights, and suggestions. For the young man who took that place after I'd had enough, the frustration of being so ignored and disrespected led him out the Church door forever, as far as I have heard.

I applied for the paid role in the church office, having volunteered with the woman now leaving the post for other opportunities. I was not even offered an interview, told the committee thought I would be better in a different job with better prospects. They may have been correct in their assessment; I may have been setting my sights within too limited a view. But it was *my* decision, my mistake to make, and it felt condescending and patronizing to be denied an interview on these grounds.

Brian Edgar observes that we "assume children are to be students, rather than teachers, of adults . . . that they need to be taught and helped by those that have already learned something of life and faith."[1] But,

> Jesus emphasized the need for adults to learn from children: "I praise you Father, Lord of heaven and earth, because you have hidden these things from the wise and learned, and revealed them to little children . . . truly I tell you, anyone who will not receive the kingdom of God like a little child will never enter it." True childishness, play, and laughter are essential parts of an authentic spiritual life.[2]

The older people "knowing better" was part of a broader problem of so-called "gate keepers" at the time. A generation of leaders who had taken over the reins and held them a long time, were finding it difficult to let go and encourage the next generation to employ *their* gifts. When you let new people in, they will change things, the ones already in leadership will lose power, influence, control. These are understandable fears, but the church (and other organizations) has not always done well to acknowledge such fears for what they are, and support people through the grief that accompanies change, towards the hope for renewal that comes from change.

The result of all that was that I felt disempowered, when I rarely had in 20 years with the Church, and I was not staying around for that.

---

1. Brian Edgar, *The God Who Plays. A Playful Approach to Theology and Spirituality.* Eugene, OR: Cascade, 2017, 20.
2. Edgar, *God Who Plays*, 23.

Intangibles

We, the church (and I am sure organizations elsewhere) exist with inherited organizational cultures. Donald E. Zimmer identifies the kind of alternative culture longed for by many within any organization. In existing organizational cultures one finds such features as a "hierarchy, top down authority," competition, task focus, military and sports metaphors, and an emphasis on knowing and answers. In "longed-for organizational cultures," one will be more likely to find a culture of servant-hood, driven from the bottom up, value for "giftedness," cooperation, relationships, "development, organic relational metaphors, learning," and questions.[3] The fuller list of contrasting word pairs Zimmer presents emerge from listening to people involved in a research project, and echo responses from research conducted by others.[4] Western culture, the culture in which I live, often privileges the qualities of governance in the first column, and marginalizes those in the second. As a result, those who long for these latter qualities in the shaping of our organizations are often not the ones enacting or shaping governance and administration; are disempowered, and voiceless.

I had started to feel disengaged from our gathered worship. Too many words, not enough silence. Too much prose, not enough poetry. Too much stiffness, not enough movement. Too busy, not still enough. (I am aware of a paradox here, too still, not still enough; not enough movement, too busy—it's a paradox, or a striving for balance that will find its way into life-giving expression in the Rule of Sacred Presence in Part Three). More often than not I was leaving worship gatherings dissatisfied, disengaged, and disillusioned; if not downright angry. So, I started taking those shifts at the bookstore, catching the train for the city at the station down the road from the building in which my church community were gathering each Sunday morning.

I am playful, an artist, if "'artist' means 'I am seeking, I am striving, I am in it with all of my heart.'"[5] I found gathered worship deeply unsatisfactory, for there was little *play* in our gathered worship—plenty of "givens", little seeking or striving. The spiritual life without play is all work, tedium, and dull.[6] Faith is imagining "what if"; play is imagining what could be.

---

3. Donald E. Zimmer. *Leadership and Listening. Spiritual Foundations for Church Governance*. Herndon, VA: Alban Institute, 2011, 145.

4. Zimmer, *Leadership and Listening*, 145–46.

5. Purnell, *Being in Ministry*, 11: citing Vincent van Gogh.

6. Edgar, *God Who Plays*, 8; 73.

Part One: Play

"Play in the spiritual realm has the same qualities that play has at any time: it does not deal with what is, but rather with what could be. It always involves another, transcendent world or sphere of meaning."[7] When we gather for worship and tell the stories, proclaim the Word of God, we act *as if* this is true, and we believe *it is* true. This enables "the believer to transcend the immediate world and experience the new" world Holy One promises and brings about.[8]

I felt disengaged: why *would* I stay?

I found my way back

While I was working in that bookshop, and later another, I was also studying English and Creative Writing at university. This was my second stint at Uni, the first being for a Bachelor of Arts with majors in French and Legal Studies, and a minor in Psychology. During that first degree, I discovered I did not want to be a child psychologist working in family courts or criminal justice, as I had planned on finishing high school.

Firstly, the workload for psychology was double that for my other subjects, and if that was a sign of things to come, no thank you. Secondly, I was experiencing Depression for the first time, and I was concerned about my capacity for the emotional stress of the career I had thought I wanted.

What I found I did want more than anything was to write. I had no idea how to make a living and write, but it was where the passion was, so I wanted to give it a go.

I got my first proper job, in the church's state (Synod) offices, secretary in the Children and Youth Ministry Units, and switched out of Psychology to French as my second major. I had to study part time to make up the missing units of French over an extra year. Then, for a year after the degree, I worked on the front reception desk a couple of days a week in addition to the days in the youth office, full time work for the first time while I sorted out what to do with my dream of becoming a writer.

Study English, I thought. Learn my craft. Some of the people with whom Dad played tennis for much of my childhood were on the English Faculty at Flinders University, where Dad worked, and I had studied already. Syd Harrex read my poetry, and thought I had enough of a gift to invest in with study at university. At the time, I planned to go on to a PhD

---

7. Edgar, *God Who Plays*, 9.
8. Edgar, *God Who Plays*, 36.

in English, and a career in University English academia. The enrolment advisor loved this idea, and with majors and good grades in language-rich subjects already, approved my unorthodox enrolment into the whole English major in one year. Normally, you can't do levels two and above before completing level one. I aced the level one topics while also achieving a high GPA across levels two and three, so I suppose the advisor's faith in me was justified. This year of studying the English major is one of a few I can recall when I was happily getting out of bed in the mornings, studying into the evening rather than mindlessly watching TV, and happy. No, deeper than "happy," I knew *joy*.

The following year, I took Honors in Creative Writing, a new program for the University. My thesis was titled "The Experience of Depression in Contemporary Australian Poetry," and my own collection of poetry on the theme alongside it was titled "Loves Labors Lost." Much later—more than ten years—many of those poems formed a large part of my debut poetry collection, *On Wisdom's Wings*.[9]

But I digress.

I was going to tell you how I wound my way back to church, wasn't I? Obviously, at some point I must have, as I am writing about finding my way as a leader in the church.

Well, writing, developing my voice as a poet and writer, was the first step.

Our congregation had a tradition at the time of putting on a play interspersed with carol singing for a family Christmas Eve service. And my mum had become one of its key facilitators. Mum was looking for a story for the next Christmas play. I had an idea. If I wrote a new play, would she consider it? Yes. And when the team chose it for that year's Christmas Eve celebrations, they also asked me to direct it. And I stepped one step back into church.

As I directed the young ones playing the shepherds, I encouraged them to take the characters and make them their own. I gave to the ones coming after me what, in another context, had not been offered to me: I welcomed and respected *their* interpretation, *their* leading in that part of the story. When the shepherds entered the church, running from their "fields" to the town to find the inn, they made their way over the pews, clambering through the people, pushing them aside, bumping up against them in their haste and their joy. One of them had brought a sheep with him—a

---

9. Sarah Agnew, *On Wisdom's Wings*. Adelaide: Ginninderra Press, 2013.

Part One: Play

stuffed toy, stuffed into the belt hiding under the outer shift, revealed in all that hustle and tumble. "The hallmark of Christian discipleship," according to Pavol Bargár, "is the faithful, yet imaginative, following of Christ here on earth." Further, "discipleship entails . . . active and deep involvement in Jesus' mission of the proclamation and embodiment of life 'to the full' (John 10:10 NIV)."[10] Could I tell you a better story of deep involvement, such embodiment of life to the full, than these young men clambering over pews, shepherds hurrying with joy to meet the new-born Jesus?

The next year, I took another step back into church, with another play. This time, I adapted a children's picture book, and again was there for rehearsals, curating photographed scenes for "flashbacks" to project on screen, and I took part on the night.

Two steps back into church.

The ministers with our congregation at that time—I still thought of it as mine with my family, even if I was hardly ever there—invited me on occasion to offer my creativity in worship. Storytelling, drama, poetry. On one of these occasions, mum and I presented the psalm for the day together. She spoke it aloud from up the back of the church with a portable microphone. Up front, I was in my bright sky-blue drama bag. These are like person-sized pillow cases, into which a person steps, pushing your hands into the top corners, and planting your feet on the ground in the bottom corners. The material has a two-way stretch, and the idea is to create strong poses within the bag to capture emotion and postures that are evoked by the stories. Our friends Carole and Rina introduced the Network of Biblical Storytellers[11] to these bags as they told stories in tandem, one speaking, one striking poses. After this particular service, one member came to me and spoke of the impact that encounter with the psalm had on her. "I don't usually remember the details of the readings we hear, but I will remember how that made me feel." And she did—months later we had another conversation about it, and the impact was still evident.

Three step, four step, five.

We have made it now to 2004. The National Christian Youth Convention (NCYC) for the Uniting Church was approaching. This was

---

10. Pavol Bargár. *Embodied Existence. Our Common Life in God*. Eugene, OR: Cascade, 2023, 20.

11. I will tell you more about the Network of Biblical Storytellers a little later on. nbsint.org

a biennial week-long event for 16–25-year-olds, with worship, speakers, bible studies, workshops, and evening concerts. Members of our congregation were helping with the organization of the Convention, which was to be held this time in Adelaide. Nancy and Peter approached me: they needed someone to coordinate the "nitelife" program—the arts and entertainment to be offered each night. *Sarah, you have worked in youth ministry, you are creative, would you coordinate the nitelife events for us?*

My first thought was that there was no way I could do that. Though I had worked for two years in the Synod youth office, helping to coordinate camps and large events, I had no idea *how* one would organize such a program. But, strangely and alarmingly, I also felt that "yes" was the answer to give. Drawing on all the contacts I had made working in the youth office, and from a lifetime in the church, I began to scout around for musicians, comedians, and visual artists. In time, a couple of other young people offered to help coordinate the program, one of whom had experience working with bands, which meant she was able to help draw up artist agreements and schedules, and liaise with the technical team. I would have been lost without Carissa.

With NCYC set for the first week of 2005, Christmas 2004 got lost in last minute details. Those early weeks of summer we put out calls for couches for our jazz lounge, and then drove around Adelaide picking them up (putting a dent in my friend's car boot with one as we lifted it down off the roof). We bought boxes of bottled water, chased notoriously disorganized artists for information (apologizing to the tech team many times), printed signs and programs, and felt the butterflies grow ever more agitated in anticipation.

Participating in NCYC from the viewpoint of nitelife was certainly very different from my only previous experience of the event as a camper (ten years earlier, the last time it was held in Adelaide). We were up late into the night, buzzing from the energy and adrenaline of last-minute hitches, pulling off our own juggling acts to reschedule artists and venues unexpectedly, and interacting with performers and campers. We slept late each morning. The days were spent replacing programs and signs around the campsite, catching a speaker's session here, chatting to campers and other team members there, then getting ready for the next round of shows with set up and sound checks.

Part One: Play

Sometimes, the Christian church does not take play seriously.[12] Is the only value in such a convention in the "work" participants do in the studies and listening to sermons? We heard above from Pavol Bargár that to be a disciple is to be faithful and imaginative. Brené Brown observes the body's biological need for play is akin to its need for rest—which we may more readily acknowledge.[13] So to nurture our disciples, we must nurture their capacity for play. Play has value in and of itself—with or without a "faith" element, a "biblical" message. Play in such a convention with its aim to grow disciples is necessary in and of itself.

But if you need more of the why for the nitelife program, play is also relational.[14] It builds community—and that is a core element of what it is to be church, is it not? To build communities of mutual encouragement (e.g., as Paul describes in his letter to the Romans), for the flourishing of all life? The church offers much, Courtney Goto observes, when we offer opportunities for play.[15] I "lead", I accompany others, with play.

Six step. Big step. Right in.

After NCYC, I found I had stepped so far back into church I started to look for ways to address the reasons I had left. In the first instance, this came in the form of a new worship service to offer at my home church. In particular, the experience of putting on a jazz lounge as part of nitelife had inspired in me a new idea for providing meaningful worship for youth and younger adults at our church. This was a question that had been asked, and variously, rarely successfully, answered, during the four or five years my family and I had been at Blackwood Uniting: the question of how to provide meaningful spaces for youth and young adults. I wondered, what if we held a jazz type church gathering?

And with that question, I was properly back in my local congregation, leading by experimenting, exploring—playing. Music, performance, experimentation, innovation. I am present as a leader through play.

---

12. Courtney T. Goto, *The Grace of Playing. Pedagogies for Leaning into God's New Creation*. Eugene, OR: Pickwick, 2016, 10.

13. Brené Brown, *The Gifts of Imperfection*, Center City: Hazelden, 2010, 101.

14. Bargár, *Embodied Existence*, 58; Goto, *Grace of Playing*, 11.

15. Goto, *Grace of Playing*, 11.

Pause

Listen to some jazz

Listen to yourself: what is stirring within?

Be curious: what are you wondering?

~

Black Wood Jazz

The church hall is set with tables and chairs. Black and white gingham tablecloths, with sticky notes and pens amongst the BYO nibbles and "good" coffee or tea we provide. Two guitarists in the corner play soft, lounge jazz, enjoying the music they are making together. In a moment, I will tell a story, something from the biblical tradition perhaps, and then we will play. As the jazz picks up again and weaves around us, we will name our questions, explore with curiosity gaps in the story, the ways this story evokes our own or contrasts with it. We will wonder. We will write or draw our questions and discoveries, our wonderings and stories, and stick them on a wall together. We will pray our thanks for stories and the Giver of the Story we follow. We will share deeply of our selves and we will get lost, with those two in the corner, in the jazz tunes they are playing to lift our souls with Spirit.

This was Black Wood Jazz.

I am a clarinetist. My clarinet is made from wood, and it is black. I have sometimes heard this instrument fondly nicknamed a "licorice stick". I like to play in a jazzy style, especially my improvised "twiddling" around the songs we sing in church. The church I called home was named for the suburb in which the building is located, as are many in our movement: Blackwood Uniting Church. So, when we started our jazz café style service, I named it Black Wood Jazz. How many apart from me understood the use of two words rather than the one name of the suburb / church, I will never know, but I liked it.

When my family moved to this congregation from another down the road, many of Blackwood's youth were moving to the congregation in which we had been most of my life. Or, to its youth group at least. While

Part One: Play

we had had enough of restricted theology, conservative and proscriptive teaching, and a growing dismissal of women and children and our contributions, some of my peers were seeking more certainty and clarity from the church and its application of the Scriptural tradition. Blackwood was, and is still nearly 30 years later, a congregation of openness and discussion, diverse ideas and perspectives, and creativity in exploring and expressing our encounters with the Sacred. This suited me. A little older than "youth" as a 20-something, used to vigorous discussion in university classrooms, refectories, and the Tavern, I wanted *that* with faith conversations, with the Bible. I had been taught how to have ideas, and I wanted to explore my ideas about Holy One. When, later, I was at theological college, I read an affirmation of this approach to starting a new thing by asking what questions you yourself have. Engage with those questions authentically, and others will join you for that.[16] There was more than one church down the road from us who gave more definitive answers for those who wanted them. We did not need to add another gathering with that approach: let's put on a gathering, create space, for those with questions they want to explore.

It took us a little while to find our groove with Black Wood Jazz. At first, we sang church songs in a jazz style. But that didn't quite feel right. We were also, in the beginning, inviting a different group of musos each time. And that didn't help build the distinct energy and atmosphere we were seeking, changing musicians and styles for each gathering. Then, we asked Tim's brother to bring his jazz guitar and a friend. As they played through our conversation, they set the tone of playful improvisation, held us in our posture of exploration and play on the well-known Song we have inherited. Pam and I caught each other's eye across the room, and shared a knowing smile. *This* is it. This is how we bring the jazz.

We experimented with space, and found that making changes with setting *was* helpful from one gathering to the next. We brought in plants and a water feature for Jesus' mountain retreats; candles and fabric created a "campfire" for a cool August night; clouds and flames were projected onto sheer white fabric hung in the center of the room for the stories of Jesus' ascension and the Pentecost visit of the Spirit. We set up a long square table for Easter with paper on which to doodle in response to the stories, and

---

16. As Riddell et al. encourage from their experiences in alternative church community building. Mike Riddell, Mark Pierson, Cathy Kirkpatrick, *The Prodigal Project. Journey into the Emerging Church*. London: SPCK, 2000, 37–38.

deck chairs in the carpark for a summertime Christmas encounter with stories of courage.

Often, I would tell by heart or read dramatically a biblical story and then pose questions, inviting the people to discuss, imagine, explore meaning for themselves—differing from the preaching way of proclaiming the Word in traditional protestant church. We would draw on tablecloths, write our own questions on sticky notes to post on boards, and of course, we lit candles, a stable act of interactive, alternative worship. We served good coffee and brought our own supper. Our team included two teenagers who shared ideas at our afternoon tea meetings, set the spaces, offered welcome, and provided our tech support. I had been leading church since I was a child: I will always invite children and youth to lead.

But, although young ones helped lead Black Wood Jazz, and I had started it *for* younger adults, rarely did any other younger adults attend. Not even the ones who had enjoyed the Jazz Lounge at NCYC. Perhaps adding the conversation and questions changed it from purely about the jazz, and it was that which they had appreciated back in the summer. We did often welcome friends of Blackwood Uniting Church members, visitors, and strangers. In this way, we were still meeting our goal to provide space that was welcoming of those on the edge of church. Further, the conversations enriched the faith of the Blackwood Uniting Church members who attended as an addition to their participation in "traditional" worship gatherings. The folk in my community seemed to appreciate this added layer, an opportunity to engage with their faith and questions in a different environment, and hear different perspectives: to wrestle with ideas, and grow, together.

"Rowan Williams asserts that the tellers and readers of the scriptural story are challenged to be much more than tellers and readers only: they are invited to become full-bodied characters in the story that has come to be theirs."[17] We are enacting the story; we are participating in a living, embodied story, and that means the story is unfolding as we go. We try, we explore, we risk, and yes, we fail. In enacting the story of the Divine's constantly renewing relationship with creation, I was also enacting the imperative for constant renewal—constant change and growth—that is part of the Uniting Church's DNA.[18] What's more, such curiosity, it turns out, is good for us,

---

17. Bargár, *Embodied Existence*, 19.

18. Uniting Church in Australia, *Basis of Union*, Adelaide: MediaCom, 1977 & 1992 (Rev. Ed.), Paragraphs 1, 3, 4, 11, 13, 14, 17, 18: with language of "pilgrim people always on the way," renewal, reform, review, learning, "fresh words and deeds," responding to God's call, guidance of the Spirit, and having been come "into being in a period of

Part One: Play

even with the disruptions it inevitably brings, for "curiosity is unruly . . . it assumes that all rules are provisional . . . It disdains the approved pathways, preferring diversion, unplanned excursions, impulsive left turns. In short, curiosity is deviant."[19] However, while it may feel destabilizing, the human "brain's chemistry changes when we become curious, helping us to learn."[20] Curiosity, exploration, *play*, is good for us.

We held a larger-than-life Black Wood Jazz one summer, with "Jazz on the Lawns" at Nunyara Conference Centre in the next suburb. A band, a theatre troupe, picnic, sausage sizzle, and a view of the sun setting over the Adelaide / Kaurna plains.

And what turned out to be our final gathering was held in Belair National Park. The story was embodied by three "actors" taking on characters from the stories of Jesus' last week before crucifixion. It was Palm Sunday. The characters moved between the tables and told their story in the actors' own words, engaging in conversation in character and not, as we all entered the story. Then we shared a eucharist together. My hope was for Black Wood Jazz to live beyond me, when I moved from Blackwood Uniting to another congregation as part of my training and formation as a candidate for ordination. But I was a leader who, not for the first or last time, failed to meet her goal.

∼

Pause

Listen to some more jazz, guitar if you can find it.

What questions are arising?

What stories of your own are you recalling?

∼

---

reconsideration of traditional forms of the ministry and the renewed participation of all people."

19. From Ian Leslie, *Curious: The Desire to Know and Why Your Future Depends on It*, cited in Brown, *Dare to Lead, Brave Work. Tough Conversations. Wole Hearts*. London, UK: Vermilion, 2018, 171.

20. Brown, *Dare to Lead*, 171.

Playing on the Edge

Failing

Sometimes the ruins are as entertaining as the castles.

Judi Dench, *Shakespeare, The Man Who Pays the Rent*

I THINK WE ARE too afraid of failure, of actually failing and being seen to fail, as if nothing is gained when something does not meet our goals or expectations. Brené Brown sees "all the dreams that we don't follow because of our deep fear of failing, making mistakes, and disappointing others. It's terrifying to risk," she observes: "your self-worth is on the line."[1]

What I mean when I say "I failed" in this instance is that Black Wood Jazz did not continue without me. I failed to successfully pass the baton so that Black Wood Jazz would live beyond my time as its facilitator. Rolf Nolasco speaks of the way our mistakes invite reflection, and thus learning, and thus growth, if we can let go of being right and perfect, and embrace being imperfect and those opportunities to learn. We can do so, Nolasco suggests, when we are not only resilient, but hopeful, because of who we are in Christ.[2] When we embrace imperfection, we also open up to "courage, compassion, and connection," states Brown; we embrace authenticity and our shared humanity.[3] For Edgar, play develops empathy through the

---

1. Brown, *Gifts of Imperfection*, 57.

2. Rolf Nolasco Jr, *Contemplative Counselor, A Way of Being*. Minneapolis: Fortress, 2011, 21.

3. Brown, *Gifts of Imperfection*, 58, 60.

Part One: Play

failing, and the making of mistakes that is intrinsic to play;[4] and Judi Dench goes even further to claim that *magic* happens when we make mistakes.[5]

My supervisor asked me if I was at peace with the possibility of failure, as I embarked on the next experiment after Black Wood Jazz. I could reply "yes" because of the hope and resilience I had learned to trust, in part, through the Black Wood Jazz experience of failure. I could reflect on the failure with Black Wood Jazz because I took a posture of play in relation to life in Christian community. Brené Brown talks of a "grounded confidence [that] is the messy process of learning and unlearning, practicing and failing, and surviving a few misses. This brand of confidence is not blustery arrogance or posturing or built on bullshit; it's real, solid, and built on self-awareness and practice."[6] I can be vulnerable enough to play and risk failing because I have nurtured, am always nurturing, self-awareness, leaning into my identity in the Holy in order that I may be grounded, confident that my self-worth is not found in being right.[7]

We held Black Wood Jazz gatherings roughly four times per year for five years. The team met monthly in the café across the road from the church, on a Friday, for afternoon tea. We would order milkshakes, coffee, or wine, and often a bowl of wedges to share. And we would plan our theme, our story, our invitations to respond, and who in the team would take on what tasks in preparation. Rowan took the lead on tech, noting what sound, lighting, and projection support we would need. Pam often offered a haiku and photo for promotion, to convey our theme. Someone would prepare the story and questions, another the milk, coffee, and tea. And someone would contact the newsletters and networks to tell people about the event.

More than once, these "someones" were all me. In a pattern that is only now beginning to abate, almost twenty years on, I would say "I can do that" more often than I asked "who can take that on?" I recall feeling so overwhelmed by all the things to do that a week out from an event, I would have made little progress on designing the set-up, let alone sourcing materials; I had no idea if we had enough coffee or tea or anyone lined up to

---

4. Edgar, *God Who Plays*, 13.

5. Judi Dench with Brendan O'Hea. *Shakespeare. The Man Who Pays the Rent.* Dublin, IR: Penguin Random House, 2023, 198.

6. Brené Brown, *Dare to Lead*, 165.

7. In "Be", I am going to tell you of a cave in which I found the depth of my trust in Holy One, found hope and my choice for life.

buy the milk, and advertising? Nobody knew we were on, or not many. My mum was on the team, and I can remember at least one Black Wood Jazz event for which she sat me down to write a list of all the things I had not done, and picked up herself many of the pieces I had dropped.

There have been seasons in which I have more readily asked for help since then. I will tell you about the PhD years later, during which I did enact the learning from such lessons as the Black Wood Jazz years provided. But in a recent placement, when we had the stress of a pandemic and various challenges within our leadership team, I again fell more than once into that unhelpful practice of taking things on myself rather than asking others to help. It can be quite a trap when others look to you for "leadership", so you feel as though you must do it all; or when your community is in crisis, everyone struggling, and you feel as though it is kinder and easier to do it all yourself. And you will not be at all surprised to learn that this recent season for me ended in burn out.

I, then, am a leader who fails. Who is fallible. Who has much to learn; who does not always implement learning as well as I would like.

Pause

Failure. What has that brought up for you?

Take a breath, go for a walk, write or paint or dance it out.

The Esther Project

The Esther Project was an experiment in forming a new faith community around the creative collaboration of staging a play in the Adelaide Fringe Festival. The Esther Project began with a pattern of weekly gatherings for a shared dinner. We met in the building of our host congregation, a younger building with kitchen and a variety of meeting spaces. I would tell part of the story of Esther from the Old Testament/Hebrew Bible, and we would wonder, imagine, probe into the gaps and connections with our own stories. If this was the story the community would tell for our dinner theatre shows at the Fringe Festival, we as a community and its members needed

Part One: Play

to know the story of Esther well, get it into our bones and sinews, our feelings and knowing. Each week, different people gathered, usually three or four others, sometimes not even that many. People rarely came back after one visit, and I never found out why. I changed from weekly to fortnightly gatherings; changed from bring something to share, to supper provided by The Esther Project (aka me). Many times, I was alone at the table, or joined by one other. And when it was only one but me, at first, I chose not to go ahead with a more formal shape to the evening. Which is when I learned something new.

I learned through this experience the importance of still holding the space as sacred, even when only one other person turned up. That person expected, was looking for, what was to be offered there. To throw it out and say, we'll just have a chat, or let's turn around and go home, does not honor their hope, their purpose in being in that place. Sure, sometimes you will read the moment and both acknowledge we might be there out of obligation and there is somewhere else we can usefully be. But sometimes, the one person before you is *wanting* the story, the prayer, the stepping out of the everyday that is promised by "church"—no matter how alternative that form of church may be. I learnt this after receiving feedback, explicitly voiced after the event, and in the body language of people who came. I felt my own disappointment when I gave in to the discomfort and reneged on the plan, when I did not hold the sacred space I had promised.

You hold that space differently for one or two others than the way you hold space for eight or a dozen, which is different again from holding space for 20, 50, 100, 1000. I could do big gatherings, no problem. Unlike the many people I encounter for whom it seems the bigger the crowd the more intimidating, for me, those numbers do not cause anxiety. What I found intimidating for a while there was to be minister, to lead in ritual, liturgy, story, prayer, *one* other person, or two. To be looked to by that one for guidance through a formal liturgy felt awkward, exposed. I learnt through error, experience, reflection, and then trying again, how to confidently hold sacred space, liturgical space, for me and one other. I am sure that has also enriched the way I am present and hold space for the gatherings of dozens and of hundreds.

Over time, we changed the pattern of our gatherings. I say "we" because a couple of interested friends did join me for a while to form a creative planning team. We met for dinner or a drink each month, and they listened, reflected, and shared decision making; and for a time, it was much more like a community. So, *we* decided to change the rhythm of our gatherings. We also decided, in time, to pull out of the theatre show and the Fringe Festival, and be, simply, a space and community for deep and creative encounter with story, Sacred and human.

Our Maundy Thursday gathering of 2010 occurred within a six-week pattern of gathering we were now following. We encountered the same story three times, each a fortnight apart. Through Lent 2010, it was the story of Jesus, anointed. Our first encounter would feature wondering and creative response. I would tell the biblical story and invite "wondering". This practice was particularly developed for Godly Play, but I and others use it in other forms of storytelling. The idea is to tell a story, then invite the hearers to respond with a brief sentence imagining—or wondering—about this or that detail, gap, emotion, character, in the story; each response begins, "I wonder." We do not answer each others' wonderings, although we might wonder something in response to another. There is no conversation at this point. The wondering simply expands into the gaps, invites connection through imagination, asks us to linger and go deeper into the emotions and senses and memories evoked by a story.

I would then tell the story again after our wondering, and those imagined details, our questions, hang in the air to enrich our second hearing of the story. I find my imagination picks out textures, details, feelings, with more rich depth on a second telling or hearing. For this first gathering with the story, we would then be invited to play—to further respond with prayerful creativity at interactive "stations", a feature of many alternative church endeavors. There might be a table full of newspapers and a prompt to find in a story of our time something that resonates with the story we have heard—cut it out, make a collage, say a prayer. There might be some poems others have composed on a theme or the actual story we have heard, and an invitation to compose your own. There would usually be a table of paper and drawing implements and the invitation to depict the story or your wonderings visually. Leaves for prayer trees, candles, themed crafts to make something to take home and remember or add to each others' responses. We would come together for some supper and share from our prayerful creativity.

Encounter 2 would begin the same with story and wondering, then move into a longer time of conversation over supper. The invitation would be to pick up on our wonderings, and to name the ways the story had travelled with us and interacted with our own stories over the intervening fortnight. We would draw our ideas together to create a third new encounter with the story in worship.

Part One: Play

Encounter 3 would be an alternative worship gathering shaped by our encounters and integrating our creative prayers and wonderings for another different entry into the story. For Maundy Thursday, this was to be a joint gathering we would lead for us and our host congregation.

If numbers of people attending matter, Maundy Thursday was our largest, at around 30 people. However, I am more interested in the impact of a gathering on those who attend than how many are there. For those who attended that Maundy Thursday, the impact lingered. People were still speaking of this gathering with wonder and gratitude months, even up to a year or more afterwards.

As I mentioned, we chose the story of Jesus anointed at Bethany, which is often told during Holy Week (the week leading into Good Friday). When we first encountered the story I brought a poem, "Woman with ointment"[8] by Jan Sutch Pickard, into conversation with the biblical story. This poem tells the story from the woman's point of view, in her voice. As people responded to the story and the poem, they wondered about Jesus' perspective, and I was commissioned to write a companion piece to bring to our second encounter with the story. I named it "Jesus, anointed, anointing".[9]

As we planned our alternative worship gathering for Maundy Thursday, we used the two poems and their conversation with the story and each other to shape the liturgy. Members of our small community took roles speaking, leading singing, providing hospitality. Worshippers were invited to wash their hands on entering the foyer. Then to take a paper cup and stick to it a word from the journey through Lent, with an invitation to share words and Lenten experiences with others over a drink and nibbles.

We sat in a circle. There were activities for children alongside. To tell the story, the poems were spoken aloud: first "Woman with ointment" by women taking a verse each in turn, then "Jesus anointed, anointing" by men doing the same. There was silence, singing, and the poems were repeated together, alternating verses from each in the same voices as before. Oil was passed around the circle, and we were each invited into the anointing.

Then the story of Jesus in the garden was told: he went to the garden, invited his friends to pray. We sang the Taizé song "Stay with me".[10] I knelt

---

8. Jan Sutch Pickard, "Woman with Ointment", in Jan Sutch Pickard, *Out of Iona. Words from a Crossroads of the World*. Glasgow: Wild Goose, 2003, 74–75.

9. Sarah Agnew, "Jesus, anointed, anointing", *On Wisdom's Wings*, 138.

10. Taizé is a Catholic monastic community in France, from which much music, mostly simple and chant-like, has emerged. taize.fr/en

by the central table, and two others extinguished candles and took away the supper elements. People were invited to stay as long as they needed, then to leave in silence. To leave Jesus in the garden alone.

Planting Seeds

So often, we have to plant the seeds in different soil to learn what grows well, where, and how to nurture life in different places. The Esther Project was a new venture in alternative church that I initiated after Black Wood Jazz. The Esther Project "failed", by some measures; and I "failed" to implement learning from the Black Wood Jazz experiences.

And although this is a story of failures, it is also a story of seeds planted, some of them in fields for growers other than me. This is the story of an endeavor that reached hardly any of its original goals, and which, even so, yielded much in the way of learning and growth, as I continued to lead, to be present, through play.

Why "Esther"?

I have not always been so clever with titles as I was with Black Wood Jazz. "The Esther Project" was a working title, from the initial goal of putting on an interactive dinner theatre production of the biblical book, *Esther*, for the Adelaide Fringe. I hoped that by doing so, I might gather artists and creatives into a community grounded in Christian faith. These were the folk I had noticed were leaving Church as we knew it, for reasons similar to my own all those years ago. Too many words. Too much prose. Not enough space. Not enough poetry. Not enough creative arts.

Esther is Hebrew Bible, and is important in storytelling rhythms of Jewish community, told annually in February or March in synagogues the world over. Purim is the festival in which Esther is told, then re-told in a Purim-Spiel (Purim-Play) such as the one I saw with an Old Testament class. "Esther, Esther, wherefore art thou Esther?" brought the biblical story into conversation with Shakespeare, and if I only ever see one Purim Spiel, this is the very one it should be.[11] Here are some thoughts I composed after visiting the synagogue for that Purim celebration.

11. I tell more about my love for William Shakespeare's work elsewhere: if I digress in that direction now, we might never find our way back. The audio album *In His House* collects many of the stories and poems I have composed in response or homage to

Part One: Play

Last night a group from the Esther Project went to Beit Shalom, the Progressive Jewish Synagogue in Adelaide, for their annual Purim-Spiel. Each year Jewish communities around the world celebrate Purim, the festival introduced in the book of Esther. The story is read aloud, with booing and hissing and rattling of noisy sound makers to drown out the name of Hamaan for all time; people dress up, and then the story is told again, this time reinterpreted in a play.

We caught the end of the telling of the biblical story, enough to witness the palpable enthusiasm with which the people were making noise at every mention of the name of Hamaan.

This year's play had a Shakespearean flavor, with MacAhasuerus, Juliester, Mordlet, and others. There was cross dressing, half a dozen plays on Hamlet's "to be or not to be," as many Shakespearean insults as could be squeezed in, and reference to most of the well-known plays and characters from the Shakespearean canon.

One of the interesting elements of critique of the story of Esther (from where I sat and I don't know if the playwright intended it as a critique), was that of the role of Vashti. MacVashti didn't disappear from the story, as she does in the Book, but was a murderous cross dresser, divorcing McAhasuerus in anger at his lack of enthusiasm for killing, and taking the identity of her cousin McHamaan in order to pursue the throne for herself.

The three witches were fabulous, stealing the show, and MacAhasuerus also did a fabulous job, keeping his accent almost to the end.

With song and dance, clever puns on well-known Shakespearean lines (including a very clever sub-plot of Gilbertstern and Rosencrantz, the only characters with "real" Jewish names but not very many lines, planning a play in which they could actually have leading roles, but who end up victims of MacVashti, who declares that Rosencrantz and Gilbertstern are dead), and humor particular to Adelaide and Beit Shalom happenings, this was a great show. I enjoyed it thoroughly, and was pleased to be invited to share with our Jewish friends the celebration of the story of Esther.[12]

Shakespeare's work. Find it at sarahagnew.com.au/shop .

12. Adapted from a post published on my former blog, sarahtellsstories.blogspot.com, 1 March 2010.

How Esther?

I chose Esther for a Fringe play because Purim coincides with Fringe Festival season in Adelaide, and what an opportunity to engage with story, conversation, play alongside our Jewish friends and their play with this story. I had spent time with the story in Hebrew language class and discovered its carnivalesque style. The features of an extravagant court and poignant if not humorous (black humor) reversals would make Esther a good Fringe Festival story, I thought.

The book is named for Esther, but begins with Vashti, Queen of the Persian court, refusing to dance before the King and his guests at their drunken party. She is actually choosing the path of least shame for both herself and her husband, for his request that she perform thus would open him to scorn and derision from the guests. However, in the moment, a moment in which his power is on opulent display, the King only feels the immediate shame of his woman's disobedience before all his subordinates.

Vashti is banished.

The King then needs a new Queen, and a somewhat farcical beauty pageant ensues. Girls are brought in from around the kingdom, into the harem, prepared with beauty treatments and proper etiquette, for their night with the King. This drawn-out pageant of girls through the King's chamber the process by which he chooses his next Queen. With extra help from the eunuch in charge of the harem, with whom we are to understand Esther has found favor, she gets the crown. I'm not sure I would say that she "won".

The court drips in opulence and power, and the story pivots on the upturning of power by the poor and the oppressed: the exiled Hebrews Mordecai and his kinswoman Hadassah, or Esther, the less foreign name by which she is known in this land. The storyteller takes pains to describe the court's adornments, pillars and curtains, tableware and thrones—of course, there is gold everywhere!

Hamaan, senior advisor to the King, is shown to be a scheming manipulator, from a nation long held as enemies to the Hebrews. He is shown up by Mordecai, whose kindness to the King is belatedly rewarded with honor Hamaan would have for himself, but is ordered to arrange for Mordecai. That old hatred is awoken, so that Mordecai becomes the target of Hamaan's vengeance, along with all Mordecai's people in the kingdom. Mordecai has advised Esther to keep her Hebrew identity a secret in the harem thus far, so Hamaan has no idea that the violence he is planning for the Hebrews in Persia includes the Queen, and will implicate him in treason.

Part One: Play

The story's opening banquet sets the scene for the later dénouement: a series of dinners at which two men with power are both brought undone, with both Hamaan's treason and the King's foolishness exposed. The King is thus brought around to grant Esther and Mordecai and their people exactly what she asks for. It is classic carnivalesque hyperbolous richesse and clever reversals. Fine storytelling fare for a Fringe Festival indeed.

As meals are such pivotal settings in the Book of Esther, I planned to set the play at a banquet, guests fed at tables while the action happened before and between them. I even planned for the guests to cause their own reversals to the story if they wished. At the climax, the guests would be presented three options for the end of the story: as it is told in the Hebrew Bible, and two new endings that claim something out of the questions and the gaps, in the finest tradition of the Jewish Purim-Spiel—Vashti returns, perhaps, or Hamaan's sons do not all get hanged with their father.

I planned that as we rehearsed the play, the creatives would wrestle with the gaps and the questions. We would tussle with this story of our inheritance, us disenfranchised Christian artists and creatives, and I would write the alternatives we would devise together through our playing with the story.

Yes, you read that correctly. I intended to write the play. My first calling was, once I got over the psychology thing, to write, if you remember. As I had remembered, all the way back to my childhood, the writer, the performer: the storyteller. My first calling was to write. So, I wanted to write the script. I wanted to gather the creatives and foster our emerging community. *And* I wanted to meet the goals of a Supervised Field Education placement for a candidate for ordination. You will be getting an inkling of where we are headed, I imagine.

I tried to recruit a director, actors, costume and set creatives. I explored partnerships: with a congregation who were very welcoming, a tech company, the publicity and funding sections of the Synod. I tried to sell the vision. People seemed interested, enthused even, but very few joined in, and even fewer took on the roles I needed others to fill. I became publicist, recruitment officer, finance and fundraising manager, pastor, *and* playwright. Not surprisingly, the script stalled in development without a director to help gather the actors and facilitate the workshops; there were few people to whom to offer any pastoral care, for the message stalled without a clear publicity campaign; and even though I found help with keeping accounts, there was hardly any money, and it hurts my brain to work with numbers.

More than the stalling of the project, the weight of the competing demands crushed me. To use such a venture as a field placement in my formation for ordination, it would have been better if we already had a script ready to go, a director and a team of volunteers for PR, fundraising, and book keeping at least all signed up. To begin such a project at all, it would have been helpful not to have a second, competing set of goals for me to have to meet, governed by their own specific time lines.

This is the nature of "fresh expressions", or pioneer ministry. These are terms the Uniting Church took from the Church of England and Methodist Church in the UK, for endeavors in Christian faith community development that break from the inherited, established, model of doing church. Pioneers are equipped and encouraged to go into the general community and build relationships, open opportunities for the meeting of people's stories with the Story of God. The aim is to respond if and when people start expressing interest in Christian spirituality and story, facilitating spiritual nurture and expression through practices authentic to the context and the people who are gathering in that place. Doing this, ministry practitioners are encountering, facing, posing questions the Church is unused to engaging with after a long era occupying a central place in the society and culture of, especially, Western countries.

Pause

Do you know the story of Esther?

Watch "One Night with the King"

Listen to David Suchet read Esther aloud—video on YouTube.

Allies

Others have written of the characteristics they observe in people who take on pioneer, or Fresh Expressions, ministry. Entrepreneurial. Charismatic.

Part One: Play

Partnered and engaged in the project together. Vision-casters. Instigators.[13] As I reflected on my choices, my strengths and weaknesses leading The Esther Project alongside these observations, I am afraid I could not see so much of myself in such descriptions. I could not see how I was a "pioneer of the pioneers" in the Uniting Church in South Australia, as I recall being introduced in a corridor at theological college. I was founder of Black Wood Jazz; biblical storyteller at many a church event; and now the founder of The Esther Project. These stories were being told throughout the church in South Australia. But all I could see was that I could not cast a vision well enough to bring others in. I could not tell this story well enough to invite financial investment. I could not. I was not.

Only

I am only, I do not know
how or what or where;

I am only, I cannot go,
I am too afraid.

I am only, I have not
height or voice or strength;

I am only, I am little,
broken, old, young.

I am only, I will not
be welcomed, heard or heeded;

I am only, they are more,
so much more than me.

I am only, but I am listening,
I will trust you when you call;

for I am only who I am,

---

13. For example, George Lings, "Looking in the mirror: what makes a pioneer?" in David Male (Ed.), *Pioneers 4 Life. Explorations in Theology and Wisdom for Pioneering Leaders*. Abingdon, UK: Bible Reading Fellowship, 2011, 30–47.

and with you I am not alone.[14]

In hindsight, a helpful concept for effective pioneering and leading generally was right there in the story of Esther itself: allies.[15] Effective pioneers need, and use, allies and advocates. Innovators and change agents may seem to be "out there" on their own, but if they are effective, they will have cultivated relationships with allies embedded in the establishment. As Esther did.

Long after The Esther Project, I built on the storytelling practice of this community, and my own practice of oral storytelling, to create a method of interpreting the bible using the body, emotion, and the performer-interpreter's relationship with her audience—essentially interpreting the Bible through play. I called the method Embodied Performance Analysis, and you can find a comprehensive introduction in *Embodied Performance. Mutuality, Embrace, and the Letter to Rome*. A step along that road was with the story of Esther. That step was an Honors thesis, in which I explored the story of Esther and Mordecai and their mutuality in leading the Jews to safety after the threats of Hamaan—and I found that they achieved this through the support of *allies*.[16] This is adapted from that Honors thesis, and concentrates on Esther 4.

> Throughout the story bearing her name, Esther utilizes what power is available to her: the power of allies and the power of emotion. The power of allies is visible in Esther's relationships with the eunuchs Hegai and Hatach. We can also observe Esther's preference for working relationally in her approach to implementing the plan she and Mordecai hatch together.[17] Esther does not prepare for her

14. Sarah Agnew, "Only", *Pray the Story*. Canberra: Self-published, 2019: 158.

15. Dave Male notes how important support and accountability are for pioneers, "because of the exposure of being on the edge" inherent in a pioneering role: "The icebergs of expectation: personal issues pioneers face," in Male, *Pioneers 4 Life*, 67–75.

16. Sarah Agnew, "The Mutuality of Esther and Mordecai: Narrative Analysis and Embodied Performance Preparation of Esther 4" (Flinders University, 2013), 72–113. Mutuality is a core commitment to which I have grown over the years: that we are fully human only together. Together with each other as humans, with the Divine Source of Being, and with all that has life. It may have been Archbishop Desmond Tutu who said we are only fully human together, but it has become such a mantra of mine, I honestly cannot remember where or when it entered my consciousness. I went on to explore its presence in the Bible again with my PhD thesis and an Embodied Performance Analysis of Romans: Sarah Agnew, *Embodied Performance. Mutuality, Embrace, and the Letter to Rome*. Eugene, OR: Pickwick, 2020, 26–28, 180–182.

17. Sidnie Ann White, "Esther: A Feminine Model for Jewish Diaspora," in *Gender*

approach to the King alone—she calls for all her people, the Jews and her servants, to fast with her, to join in solidarity, responding to crisis with positive action, *together*.

Emotion is a power that dominant powers allow their subordinates because they mistakenly regard emotion as an impediment to success.[18] Esther demonstrates that she knows the King, and understands how to manipulate his emotions to achieve her goal.[19] While some see in Esther here a movement from powerless to powerful,[20] I suggest that Esther moves from powerless to empowered.[21] It is a self-determination without which Esther could not cultivate allies, adapt, and survive, let alone thrive, as a captive participant in the King's pageant search for a new Queen. Mutuality is not self-deprecation or -denial, and is not self-determination *over* another. Mutuality is, rather, a deep honoring of the dignity and worth of the other as bound up in my own dignity and worth; and I cannot honor one if I do not honor the other.

Now I explore that mutuality as Esther expresses it through trust in allies, and will take Hatach as an example of these helpful relationships. I employ the tools of Embodied Performance Analysis, allowing emotion, intuition, and the body to act as tools for interpretation.

In 4:5 "Esther called for Hatach." That Esther calls for *Hatach* raises several questions for me in performance. Is he called on for his role, which allows him particular access to the gate and square? That another attendant has obviously already crossed to the gate with clothes between them (4:4) suggests Hatach does not have unique *access*. Perhaps, then, for the conversation that she must have with her uncle, Esther particularly trusts *Hatach*?[22]

and Difference in Ancient Israel, ed. Peggy L Day (Minneapolis: Fortress Press, 1989), 173.

18. White, "Esther: Feminine Model", 168; Angeline Song, "Heartless Bimbo or Subversive Role Model?: A Narrative (Self) Critical Reading of the Character of Esther," *Dialog: A Journal of Theology* 49, no. 1 (2010). Song describes a "subtlety of the powerless," which she sees Esther employ. Esther acts from a position of vulnerability with subversive wisdom, using her knowledge of the King and court to speak and act rarely but with devastating effect (65–67).

19. White, "Esther: Feminine Model," 168.

20. Jon D. Levenson, *Esther, Old Testament Library* (London: SCM Press Ltd, 1997), 82.

21. For Costas (Orlando E. Costas, "The Subversiveness of Faith: Esther as a Paradigm for a Liberating Theology," *Ecumenical Review* 40, no. 1 (1988), 69), the Book of Esther continues to live "in the memory of oppressed and powerless people in every society," its heroes offering a story of hope in the face of injustice.

22. I am informed in this line of questioning by the imaginative filling of gaps

Such silence, or narrative gaps, regarding motivation are a feature of this story. Indeed, "part of the artistry of the book is its knack for making us ask" questions, most posed in relation to Esther and Mordecai.[23]

Wrestling with the questions posed by such gaps is necessary for decisions regarding how and what my body will communicate. Posture and expression as I present Esther's call to Hatach will communicate my understanding of the relationship, to me first in rehearsal, then with my listeners. Subtleties of tone will represent that relationship as either a formal arrangement or a trusting friendship. I see the characterization of Esther as inspiring trust and loyalty:[24] it would not be consistent for me to adopt a tone of cool authority here. It would rather be consistent with my understanding of Esther's character throughout the entire story to employ a tone suggesting that in this hour of need she is calling on a friend, or ally, whom she trusts, and who trusts Esther in return.

Hatach is depicted going "out to Mordecai, to the city square in front of the King's gate" (4:6), and this highlights the reason Esther cannot go herself to be with Mordecai, and her need for Hatach as her ally. The city square, the King's gate, are not sites occupied by women in these stories and the culture and times they depict. As a court servant, Hatach, however, is able to cross between Mordecai and Esther, between the open court and the closed chambers of the Queen. Note my physical response when speaking the words in 4:1, "When Mordecai learned all that had been done, Mordecai tore his clothes and put on sackcloth and ashes, and went through the city, wailing with a loud and bitter cry." I gesture with my fists closed around the imagined vertical bars of a locked gate, and then shake them as if shaking that gate in frustration and anger. Perhaps frustration in part at Mordecai's separation from his kin?

We witness Esther's capacity to build relationships of mutual trust in the Palace earlier in the story. In the harem, Esther "pleased" Hegai (the head eunuch in charge of the Harem) with her kindness (2:9), and "won the favor of all" (2:15). Esther evoked kindness from Hegai, who "gave Esther beauty treatments" (with

---

by Tommy Tenny with Mark Andrew Olsen, *Hadassah. One Night with the King* (Minneapolis, MN: Bethany House, 2004).

23. Carol M. Bechtel, *Esther, Interpretation* (Louisville, KY: John Knox Press, 2002), 45. Gordis (Robert Gordis, "Studies in the Esther Narrative," *Journal of Biblical Literature* 95, no. 1 (1976) : 45) attributes these gaps, particularly noting the absence of motives for Esther and Mordecai, to the fast pace of the narrative.

24. Agnew, "Mutuality of Esther and Mordecai," 66–73.

the implication that this is beyond what is given to the others), "carefully chosen foods," dedicated servants and the best room in the harem (2:9). Esther trusted Hegai, asking for nothing except what Hegai advised (2:15) in preparation for her night with the King. It is easy to imagine into the gaps that Esther has likewise been kind in Hatach's presence, evoked kindness of Hatach, and built mutual trust to the point of Hatach's carrying dangerous messages from the Queen's chambers through the King's gate.

In embodied interpretation, as I inhabit these scenes, my body instinctively moves from my "gate side" to my "palace side,"[25] making real the space between Mordecai and Esther. My body then visually supports the movement Hatach makes at the narrator's hand into the shadows: as the narrator ceases to name Hatach's movement and speaking, so I simply turn my body rather than take steps. Thus, Esther and Mordecai seem to speak directly, though we know they are still separated by distance—a distance their ally crosses for them, facilitating *their* alliance in meeting and overcoming Hamaan's threat. In this, not only does the narrator heighten the drama and intensity of the conversation as it moves towards Esther's courageous decision to approach the King uninvited on behalf of her people; the narrator also gives the audience a glimpse into the mutuality of these relationships. Not only that of Esther and her uncle Mordecai, who are used to working things out together. The audience is invited to see them working their response out together here through another relationship of mutual trust in action of great risk to each. Faithful allies, Hatach and the servants risk their lives participating in Esther and Mordecai's own allied, and subversive, acts of resistance.[26]

An ally rises

Allies and allyship are seeds planted in me through the Esther Project. Experience, which grew and yielded fruit many years later. When I consider what allies might help a pioneer leader in the church venturing out from how things are, I will admit, 15 years later, I think, "Someone who

---

25. "Blocking" a scene for storytelling performance, a storyteller will determine where characters are standing, in which direction is the gate and the chambers of the Queen, and in order to effectively transport the audience to the story's location, consistently refer to those locations with her own eyes, gestures, and movement.

26. Linda M. Day, *Abingdon Old Testament Commentaries: Esther.* Nashville: Abingdon Press, 2005, 87–88.

might have done for me what I have done for Lauren Harkness and the Rise Community."

2020. Canberra. First lockdown of the Covid 19 pandemic. I receive a message from Lauren, who I do not know, and who is even newer to Canberra than I am. Lauren is seeking ways to connect with a fledgling community of women she's gathered over a couple of years, though scattered around Australia, for retreats and other gatherings. Lauren plans to go live on the socials every day in May, for 30 days of mindfulness. Lauren has discovered through mutual friends my blog Pray the Story, and likes what she has found there of my prayerful poetry (or poetic prayers).[27] Lauren wants to ask my permission to use some of my prayer-poems for this Mindful May series of live videos. She will acknowledge my authorship, point people to the blog and book—oh! Can she buy a copy of the book, please?

I say yes to using the prayer-poems, and to the book purchase, and as she is in Canberra, I offer to drop her copy to her house. The first time we see each other it is through two windows, her lounge, my car, after I have turned around and started back for home, having left the book by her front door. I can still see her in my mind's eye, standing at the window waving as her children will in the coming years, when I will have been welcomed into Lauren's home and friendship.

Because, months later, when we were out of lockdown, Lauren contacted me again. Could we meet in person, at last? You seem like someone I could partner with, in conversation at least, exploring new ways of being church. Sure, I said. And as we sat outside the café drinking coffee for the first of so many occasions, it felt like we had known each other for ever. You know the feeling, when you meet a kindred spirit (thank you *Anne of Green Gables* for that most excellent phrase)? As Lauren told me the story of Rise Retreats, events, and community, I somehow knew I would partner with her. The kindred thing, perhaps, or a Spirited thing, or probably both. But I knew. Lauren and I had the same question to pose—how? What might it look like for me to support Lauren and Rise?

Firstly, would I be guest poet at an afternoon tea in Berriman in the NSW Southern Highlands, for her community of women? Alison Ware would play harp music, we would sit outside on a late spring afternoon and enjoy tea, champagne, cakes . . . and my poetry, if I agree. I agreed.

---

27. Pray the Story—the blog—is no longer active. I tell more of the story of this project and its different seasons a little later.

Part One: Play

Second, we explored where my gifts and experience might meet the current needs of Lauren's ministry through Rise. The most pressing, Lauren felt at the time, was a physical home for Rise, for the events and the community. She had been, as many entrepreneurs do, operating this enterprise from home thus far. My position in the Uniting Church as a Minister of the Word placed me ideally for connecting Lauren to someone who might help. Our Presbytery had a person in a placement dedicated to looking for innovation and growth in the church; looking for emerging, fresh ways of being church and encouraging, equipping, nurturing them into their flourishing. This nurture of fresh expressions is a key focus of the Presbytery and Synod (local region and state), so let's ask the Uniting Church to live out their stated goal, I suggested.

I contacted our Presbytery Minister and gave a brief outline of Rise and Lauren's desire to make a physical home for this emerging community. Then I introduced them, and Andrew committed to supporting Lauren with his own advocacy in councils and committees with capacity to resource and support. He put Lauren in touch with a number of churches either vacant or with congregations keen for their space to be used by other community groups. Andrew offered his own support, time, presence—he met regularly with Lauren for the next two years, and connected her with growth and formation and funding opportunities. Through Andrew, the Presbytery negotiated a partnership agreement with Lauren to have a home in a building formerly home to a Uniting Church congregation.[28]

It happens that this congregation was in the parish I was serving: I had been the one to conduct the closure service, welcome the few remaining members to the continuing congregation in the next suburb, and support them through that transition. As Rise made St Aidan's church home, renaming it Sanctuary, I encouraged Wesley Uniting Church to support Lauren and the Rise community.[29] To view this new use of the building as a continuation of the story the congregation had told for over 50 years. New growth from seeds planted after the former flowers had lived their life, or been transplanted.

---

28. In time, Andrew and Lauren, with others, would collaborate to form a new community of faith called Tent.

29. Rise still exists, as Rise Events—Lauren's Event management business: riseevents.com.au. These days, the community of women supporting each other and exploring life and faith gathers under the name "At Her Table"—athertable.com.au. Sanctuary has developed a life of its own as a bespoke venue for events, photography, well-being, and celebratory gatherings: sanctuarycanberra.com.au.

Wesley members cleaned and painted, turned up for blessings, prayed, donated paint and money and more. Not formally part of the parish, Sanctuary is nevertheless part of Wesley's neighborhood, on the doorstep of many members who live locally, and it needs its neighbors' support if it is to thrive.

Linking an emerging faith community with the established church; connecting pioneer leaders with mentors, advocates, supporters; participating in the life of the community so as to know the story and tell it where you go. This is the allyship I had needed all those years ago with The Esther Project, which I did not find, nor know (how) to seek.

As my involvement with Rise deepened, I took on a role as Chaplain (later Spiritual Director) for the community. I would be Lauren's chaplain, collaborator, confidante. I would compose prayers and liturgies for the gathering of the community. I would write reflections, and later, help develop the training and support of leaders emerging in the community to lead Rise gatherings such as At the Table (conversation about the deep stuff of life), and Selah (sacred rest and creative practice), in their locations across Australia. I spoke at church meetings to advocate for financial support for Rise or to encourage people to get involved. I told the story to colleagues, and held my own events at Sanctuary to invite more people into the space. With clear intention, I was, with Andrew and a number of others, the ally for Lauren others didn't quite manage to be for me in the days of The Esther Project.

I did have people supporting me—I wasn't all alone. Some even spoke for me, helped with strategy, funding, and connections. But no one bought into The Esther Project who had a position in the church that placed them ideally to advocate, to tell the story, to facilitate the established church's effective support of The Esther Project. And it suffered for that lack.

I wonder how important it is, having someone who has *done* fresh expressions of church alongside one who is doing it now? I have done the posing of questions the church's foregoing generations have not asked; I have done and been the challenge to the church that is an unfamiliar way of doing and being church. I know some of the questions, or kinds of questions, Rise might both face and pose; I know how it feels to create that awkwardness for the establishment. To struggle, to suffer, even, in the enacting of a call you cannot ignore.

I have experienced from different perspectives the discomforts of fresh expressions of church. I have been the practitioner. I have been on committees seeking to help the church support practitioners with finance, encouragement, policy. I have been on a support team for two practitioners in Scotland, walking beside them as they led new communities in alternative shapes of church.

When I was a pioneering practitioner looking for support, hardly anyone had done this kind of thing for such a long time. Not in this context, this generation, with this intention to do and be church in a fresh way, alongside and within the established church. There wasn't a "Sarah" (or "Andrew") to my "Lauren", when I started The Esther Project. I didn't have examples of experiments in doing church differently, I only had examples of tired, worn-out congregations doing things the way things had been done for generations, and finding no younger people coming in to take over and keep it going just the same for another generation.

We did, however, and still do, tell stories from the UK context, but that can feel so far away from here. And of course, the Church of England has a very different relationship with the wider English society and fabric of life than the Uniting Church, or any church, does in Australia. There's a robustness to the Church of England, so woven into life and society, that has enabled a more courageous embrace of the need to change. Their roots are centuries deep, they can afford to bend with the breeze. Here, when we suggested the way church was being done was not working, it was received as criticism, a judgement of failure, and pushed people further into the fear they were experiencing with the dwindling numbers of members in their congregations. Fear that a new wind blowing would take the whole field down. But we are drawn into God's story, and God's story is a story of transformation and renewal,[30] and the Uniting Church is part of the Reformed Church, always reforming.[31] Although the Divine Presence is constant, if it has life, everything is *always* changing. New seeds are always falling and germinating in the depths . . .

---

30. Bargár, *Embodied Existence*, 10.

31. A commitment to renewal is discernible in almost every one of the 18 chapters of our founding document, *The Basis of Union*.

Pause

Where have you encountered the term "ally"?

What stories are emerging?

Listen. Pay attention. Be curious.

Growth rather than "outcomes"

Remember my supervisor asked me to properly find peace with the possibility of "failure" in The Esther Project? Well, I am glad I did, because The Esther Project lasted less than two years. But during that time, we did find a rich pattern of gathering around deep, imaginative connection with the story.

Almost every time we gathered, someone wrote a poem in response the story we were exploring, and often having rarely if ever written poetry before. Three poems composed at Esther Project gatherings were accepted in an anthology published by The Effective Living Centre.[1] That Centre is a community connection enterprise of the congregation with which we partnered, connecting with family life workshops, justice forums, and a regular poetry evening. Poetry writing is always an outcome I welcome, and I hope it is a practice to which The Esther Project participants have returned from time to time. That would be a worthwhile seed to plant, if we achieved nothing else.

When I remember accurately, I know we did achieve much. And we planted many seeds I am sure I haven't seen fall, or grow. Which calls to mind various parables (or stories) Jesus told.

> Then Jesus said, "This is what God's kingdom is like. It's as though someone scatters seed on the ground, then sleeps and wakes night and day. The seed sprouts and grows, but the farmer doesn't know how. The earth produces crops all by itself, first the stalk, then the head, then the full head of grain. Whenever the crop is ready, the farmer goes out to cut the grain because it's harvesttime." (Mark 4:26–29, CEB)[2]

---

1. Jude Aquilina, John Pfitzner, & Russell Talbot (Eds), *Season of a New Heart*, Adelaide: The Effective Living Centre, 2010: "Silence", Bob Macintosh (56); "The round table", Michelle Coram (72); "Off the edge" and "The deepest and the best", Sarah Agnew (92, 101).

2. See also Luke 8:4–8; 13:18–19; Matt 13:3–9.

A seed that fell and grew during our time together was in the inspiration for giving of oneself. One of our core group withdrew after a time of deep involvement with us, because she had felt the encouragement *of* our group to participate in Habitat for Humanity. Getting alongside communities in places like Nepal to build houses for people in need, and telling the story of the experience: fruit that planted seeds of hope for more than we could count.

For me, much of what worked and did not work with The Esther Project scattered seeds that also grew fruit. There has been advocacy and support for Lauren and other pioneering church practitioners in the years since The Esther Project. In Part Two: Tell, I will tell you about the claiming of my vocation as storyteller-poet-minister: those Esther Project years and experiences certainly contributed much to that emerging understanding of vocation and identity. For now, some of those playful, storied seeds from what became a storytelling community.

Playing with story

The way I engage with story, biblical story in particular, continues to emerge from this story-shaped experiment in Christian worship and community. I am finding in my practice and that of others, in engaging with and interpreting biblical compositions, a more intentional use of imagination. I will use the example of Romans and just three of us who employ imagination to interpret the letter in its hearing. Paul says only this of Phoebe:

> I commend to you our sister Phoebe, a deacon of the church at Cenchreae, so that you may welcome her in the Lord as is fitting for the saints, and help her in whatever she may require of you, for she has been a benefactor of many, and of myself also.

From that, Paula Gooder, Shola Adegbite, and I, have imagined Phoebe having carried the letter from Paul to the churches in Rome.[3]

Gooder's novel *Phoebe* gives her a back story of some trauma, fills out the scenes of streets and homes in the city of Rome, and introduces us to some of the others Paul names, and some he does not, who belong to the church there. For Gooder, Phoebe herself does not speak the letter aloud;

---

3. Paula Gooder, *Phoebe. A Story*, London: Hodder & Stoughton, 2018; Shola Adegbite, "The Story Must Go On: Biblical Storytelling as Unfinished Business", NBSI Scholars Seminar, 30 July 2024; Agnew, video 24 "Phoebe's story and Rom 12–15, Uniting College preview", sarahagnew.com.au/embodied-performance.

Part One: Play

there is one in the community who is a trusted reader aloud of scripture and correspondence. Phoebe is a listener along with the community of the church in Rome; an active listener further connecting the hearers with the sender of the letter.

Adegbite imagines Prisca and Aquila, whom Paul mentions a few verses after the commendation of Phoebe, and some in their household, listening as Phoebe speaks the letter aloud. She gives them back stories, how Prisca defied her parents in marrying Aquila, a freed man; others who are slaves or freed persons. This work of imagination helps Adegbite to give context to hearers of the letter in Rome, and how the letter might have been received, what meaning it might have offered. This is the kind of work historical, socio-critical, feminist, liberation theologians are always doing—Adegbite claims the work of imagination explicitly, where biblical scholarship has often pretended it is rational, objective, exact. Adegbite is asking—*what if?* What if Aquila was a slave who worked for his freedom, and his wife Prisca had been socially his superior? How then do they hear Paul's words, as affirmation perhaps of the choices they make as aligning with the way of Jesus? Intentionally asking *what if?*, the interpreter allows for multiple possible interpretations, liberating herself from the burden of being right with the one, correct, answer. From their earliest days, sacred compositions have been interpreted with what ifs, especially the Hebrew Bible by Rabbis through their Midrash.

I also have imagined a story for Phoebe, as did Gooder. But, with Adegbite, I put the letter in Phoebe's voice and body, on arriving in Rome. Gooder and I had both engaged in rigorous scholarship, examined the evidence as it pertains to the letter writing practices of the time; Gooder preferred the voice of one belonging to the community of hearers to speak the letter aloud, while I fleshed out a story of Phoebe having been present as Paul composed the letter. For me, that made sense, for then she can be his voice, having been part of the conversations during composition, hearing the broader arguments and philosophies of Paul first hand, to be able to give voice to, to embody in her person, Paul, which it is said letter carriers in the first century were understood to do.[4]

---

4. Kathy Ehrensperger is one who understands Phoebe to have been the letter's carrier and speaker (*Paul and the Dynamics of Power: Communication and Interaction in the Early Christ-Movement*. Library of New Testament Studies. Edited by Mark Goodacre. London: T. & T. Clark, 2007, 54), while Bernhard Oestreich agrees with Paula Gooder, that Phoebe would not have spoken the letter aloud in Rome (*Performance Criticism of the Pauline Letters*. Translated by Lindsay Elias and Brent Blum. Biblical Performance Criticism Series 14. Eugene, OR: Cascade, 2016, 73).

Again, that these interpretations are offered explicitly as works of imagination—imagination grounded in academic scholarship—invites expansive reading of the sacred texts of a faithful church. Artists—poets, storytellers, painters, sculptors, composers—have been interpreting the Bible since its stories were first composed. For some, these "receptions" are not quite interpretation in the way of scholarly exegesis; this is a misunderstanding and a dismissal of the work of the artist, the work of imagination. All scholars are using their imaginations to make sense of the evidence they find; what's more, all scholars are using their emotional and intuitive sensibilities, their bodies, their relatedness to others and creation and God, to make meaning in and through the biblical compositions. I suggest we gain more by acknowledging and listening to our bodies and imaginations than by perpetuating the false idea that we can make meaning through pure objectivity.

Embodying the story

Remember the people leaving Jesus in the garden on Maundy Thursday 2010, with The Esther Project? I did, when I was invited to take part in a Palm Sunday telling of the Holy Week stories on the streets of Edinburgh five years later. As gardener in Greyfriars' kirkyard, Pilate on the Castle forecourt, Mary mother of Jesus on the St Giles Cathedral steps, Mary Magdalene, Caiaphas, Judas, and Peter in courtyards, and finally Jesus on the site of executions during the Reformation's religious persecutions, a group of us took on characters from the scenes of Holy Week and told "our" stories. I suggested the people be encouraged to leave Jesus (me) at the Grassmarket, beneath Edinburgh Castle; that ancient site of religious crucifixions. Alone. On both occasions, this drawing people into the betrayals of many of Jesus' followers and friends, by themselves leaving him alone, had a profound and enduring impact.

Worship, when I can manage it, will be immersive and embodied for the people who gather with me. I will engage their senses, their bodies, their emotions. I will collaborate with others, bring in multiple voices, and use movement, silence, and music to tell the story, not only words. When I use words, they will often be poetic, full of imagery and emotion and space between.

Embodiment became a tool for interpreting the Bible in the new method I developed in a PhD at the University of Edinburgh. Because I had *felt* the way we interpreted, we understood, the story in moments like that Maundy Thursday walking away from Jesus.

Storied liturgy

I do not know how many, but many people in many countries and Christian traditions have now purchased and used the liturgy we composed for Maundy Thursday, published in Jan and my names.[5] At the same time this was published by Wild Goose Publishing, so were two Easter resources, all published as e-liturgies. *Walking to Emmaus Again* is another embodied and active liturgy using movement and poetry, which I developed in collaboration with Subtle Bricks drama group and Rev Sandy Boyce, for Pilgrim Uniting Church, Adelaide. *The Best of All Possible News* is three monologues from Jesus' friends after his resurrection, which I composed for Black Wood Jazz. I have used this again, notably at a dawn Easter Day service beside a river, before a fish-in-pita bread breakfast. I still remember the eeriness of driving through pre-dawn streets of Adelaide, the anticipation that hung in the stillness of the air, and the sun, rising over the Mount Lofty Ranges as we heard the stories, prayed, and sang. Since then, I have also published liturgical stories for Good Friday and Christmas,[6] this developing craft growing from the storied liturgy we crafted in The Esther Project. I "lead", I accompany others, by playing with the Sacred Stories.

Story holder

I mentioned the request from the Esther Project group for me to compose a new poem as part of our response to the story during Lent. This was seen to be part of the work I was doing between our gatherings. After we gathered, I would write a blog post that drew together some of our wondering, creative responses, connections to stories we were living. There was an art to this, for I sought to honor each person's story as theirs and not actually tell it in my voice or in that public space. It was an art of collating and alluding. But participants seemed to appreciate the way these posts still managed to reflect back to them what had been shared; they felt heard with such reflection.

---

5. Sarah Agnew and Jan Sutch Pickard, *With Intuition, Imagination, and Love.* Glasgow: Wild Goose, 2016.

6. *Survey the Cross; Tell Me the Story of Christmas.* sarahagnew.com.au.

Knowing this was a gift I could offer, the listening and reflecting back of people's sharing of themselves and their stories, I have done so in varied ways ever since.

In September and October 2015, with St Augustine's Church in Edinburgh, I facilitated a series of workshops and was then storyteller in residence for the subsequent series of performance café events as part of the Scottish Mental Health Arts and Film Festival. The theme was passion. I had been invited to work with clients of a mental health drop-in to help them identify, craft, and prepare to present, their stories of passion. Each workshop invited reflection on passion, the things we are passionate about. Each workshop included activities to nurture skills in crafting story, and offered opportunity to practice sharing our work and stories, and listening attentively to each other. I took the part of participant, myself, composing the story "In His House", remembering my pilgrimage to the home of William Shakespeare.[7] The buzz in our breaks and after each workshop, the visible lift in the demeanor of participants, were all signs to me that in these spaces people were connecting, feeling heard, affirmed, and encouraged. As the workshop participants and I shared our stories in the café events, others were inspired to return the next week (there were five altogether), with stories or poems or songs of their own passions. The sharing of stories nurtures and connects people, and evokes stories from each other; the sharing of stories strengthens individuals and communities.

Another time, I worked with a Kirk session in the west of Scotland. I led a one-day retreat in which they explored the gifts and needs of their congregation and the gifts and needs of the broader community, and discerned how they could prioritize their resources and energy towards meaningful and sustainable mutual encouragement of congregation and community.

In a later season back in Australia, I began to be sought out for mentoring, Spiritual Accompaniment, story coaching, and an emcee who listens to the stories of other presenters and composes poems that hold the stories and their hearers in the moment of encounter and shared meaning-making.[8] These roles, again, offer that gift of holding story with others, to facilitate meaning-making. This seed from The Esther Project continues to produce varied fruit well over a decade later.

---

7. Sarah Agnew, "In His House", *In His House*, 2016. soundcloud.com/sarahtellsstories/in-his-house

8. See these blog posts for some of those poet-emcee moments: sarahagnew.com.au/art-for-the-voice/; sarahagnew.com.au/hope-arising/

Part One: Play

~

Pause

I wonder: The Esther Project lasted two years. Its fruit is growing and planting its own seeds well over a decade later. Do we—the church in particular, but all generally—need a rethink on what it means for a project to be "successful"? What makes it worthwhile?

What even does it look like for a project to endure?

Do we need to move away from "failure" towards an embrace of *play*?

Can we simply say: We played. That play ended. And the play goes on.

~

Play: embodied and costly

THE RISK OF "FAILURE" is one element of play. It is a risk. It is a cost. To leap and *not* fly does hurt us in many ways: disappointment, shame, blame, consequences of errors of judgement, feeling let down. If that is not enough, play comes with costs beyond "failure".

In "Tell", I share more about the end of The Esther Project. Missed opportunities, conflicting demands, combined with the lack of the sort of allies I have talked about in earlier pages, all combined to bring an end to The Esther Project before it needed to close. And that certainly felt like failure. I felt unseen and unsupported, vulnerable on the edges of church exploring new ways to be. It was not the last time I would pay dearly as I followed the Dream, the call to play.

off the edge

as I step off the edge
of this well worn map,
which has served me well
and got me this far,
though it can take me
no further,
I wonder,
how will I find my way
from here?
as I keep walking,
tentatively,
but with no thought of turning
back,
I notice a companion
beside me
as we begin to talk,
this Presence changes

Part One: Play

sometimes speaking a lot
sometime listening deeply,
sometimes wandering off the path
in pursuit of something intriguing—
I follow, and we create a new
path to tread
as we rest beneath an ancient tree
it occurs to me
not once have I felt lost
travelling off the map—
curious, adventurous,
uncertain, and sometimes lonely,
but always found
on this untrod
unmapped path
and as we find our way
it seems others
are also venturing off the map
to try the untried
guided by a relationship
that cannot be bounded
by neat black lines[1]

If we are talking about "play", then the PhD experience was three years dedicated to it! Three whole years to play with my storytelling practice and discover if there was a method to draw out of it. Three years to experiment with embodiment and performance as a way to interpret—even more, to offer rigorous scholarly exegesis—on biblical compositions.

I have quoted from my Honors thesis on Esther already. In that work, I engaged in a narrative analysis of Esther 4, then began to make comment from the perspective of a performance of the story. As I described later in the doctoral work, this is a common approach in Biblical Performance Criticism, the stream of biblical scholarship that explores the Bible through the lens of performance as its origins and a continuing practice. Many

---

1. Sarah Agnew, "off the edge", first published in Aquilina et al. (Eds) *Season of a New Heart*, 92.

scholars within this stream undertake a narrative analysis of a passage, then shape their storytelling performance according to that interpretation.[2]

I did not feel that this is what I was doing in my storytelling performances. I did not analyze the composition then prepare it for oral storytelling performance for gathered listeners. I took the words and laid them out in short lines of sense or rhythm, printed it, then jumped straight into speaking, hearing, feeling it in my sinews, breath, and bones. In this way, I invite the composition to speak to me directly, as it is with its words and spaces. I allow my body to move, my emotions and intuition to feel, my imagination and intellect to wonder: rather than thinking and analyzing first, I begin with feeling, with play.

Then, I note the questions that arise, practicing the wondering I do with groups of listeners. To explore the questions, I might go to the Greek or Hebrew and translate anew. I might employ narrative, rhetorical, historical, feminist or other methods of interpretation. I might engage with what other scholars have thought. I might explore the tellings of other performers, or art, or music. That might shape the words I speak, so I write the "script" again, and learn the story (or poem or letter) again. And my body and emotions and the audience for whom I tell in rehearsal imagination and live performance, all continue to show me meaning in the text. Three years to play with all of this. Of course, there is so much more to that process, and I invite you to read *Embodied Performance. Mutuality, Embrace, and the Letter to Rome* if you want that story.[3]

What I don't tell in that book, however, is the story behind the PhD. The other ways I played, which subtly and overtly influenced my PhD play and work. The people with whom I collaborated and danced, lived and laughed. The cost I paid. For they were three rich *and* costly years, those years of play in Edinburgh.

I embarked on this PhD without a full scholarship. Yes. I left Australia for a PhD on the other side of the world with enough money to last six months. In another season, you might recall, I had *not* been willing to leave Adelaide for the other side of the country without a scholarship, to take up a PhD place in Perth to study Shakespeare. When anyone asks me about doing a PhD, whether they should or not, I tell them: Do it if you have a project about which you are passionate. Whether with or (especially) without the money, you need the passion and commitment to stay the course.

---

2. Agnew, *Embodied Performance*, Chapter 2.
3. Agnew, *Embodied Performance*.

Part One: Play

Perhaps because through my childhood we were surrounded by PhD students through Dad's work as administrator of the University department that looked after overseas graduate students and scholarships, I was always sure I would do a PhD. Over the years, I had dozens of ideas of things I *could* have studied, from Shakespeare to Bible. The English PhD was to have explored Shakespeare's identity in Australia: who he is to us, if he is the "bard of our idolatry" in Britain, and lover, rogue, source of intrigue for Hollywood? I even toyed with ways to study Shakespeare and the Bible together. I managed to get Shakespeare in to my eventual thesis, obliquely, as I drew on the wisdom of Shakespearean actors for their insights into embodied interpretation, and interpretation through and with their audiences. Finally, though, I had found a project that was far less about the degree and much more about the project itself. I was at last more interested in the questions I wanted to play with and explore, than the piece of paper at the end of it. The question of Australia's relationship with William Shakespeare had been interesting to me, but it didn't engage my passion, my devotion.

A lot of people and organizations helped me over those three years in Edinburgh. I got a job tutoring Mathematics and English with school students, the oldest tutor in the center by a decade, though the others were generous in their welcome of me even so. My PhD supervisors gave me the extra classes to tutor in the undergraduate courses in second year when we were allowed to take them on. I was an experienced teacher when I arrived in Edinburgh, having taught at Uniting College in Adelaide soon after graduating my bachelor degree. They also knew I had few options for other sources of income. As an Australian at that time I was ineligible for the usual Commonwealth scholarships, along with students from other wealthier countries in the Commonwealth. I understood the need for the prioritizing of support for students from developing nations; and my privilege showed out, I suppose, in the networks on which I was able to draw. I was also ineligible for the kinds of loans available to students from the USA, for which I am actually grateful, as such loans are generous at the time, and unforgiving in the burden they become for decades afterwards. So, I cobbled together small scholarships from New College School of Divinity at Edinburgh, Uniting Church sources including Uniting College, and even one from a Catholic source. A generous person was able to lend me the money to cover my final year of rent, which alleviated the stress enough that ME/Chronic Fatigue symptoms also significantly abated (I tell you more about that later). This enabled me to finish within three years, the minimum for a PhD, and a rarity.

The other way people helped me financially was through Patreon. This is a crowdfunding platform that differs from others that existed at the time. Most of those platforms allowed a creator to gather support for their next big project, such as an album or exhibition or book, from their supporters. Depending on the amount of your pledge, the artist would give you the album or book, tickets to events, exclusive merchandise and other rewards. Patreon recognized the artists who create small projects or ongoing work, and allowed the crowd to support them, too. Pledges were "per piece" (video or artwork or song), or per month; bonuses were works, behind the scenes photos and videos, exclusive previews, early bird access.

I realized that there were people in Australia willing to support this PhD project. Some were giving my mum money to send to me. What if the storyteller-poet-minister playing with the Bible and how we engage with it faithfully as a church offered a newsletter, stories, videos of the rehearsing? Would those be bonus enough for those who wanted to help? It seems they were, for a good number of folk signed up with monthly pledges, and some months I only ate because of them.

Pray the Story—beginnings

Wherever I told the story of my PhD, it was met with enthusiastic welcome. Wherever I took my poems and stories and encouraged the stories of others, I was warmly welcomed and often invited back again. My Scottish sojourn was instigated by the pursuit of a PhD, but it gave me a chance to immerse myself in a culture of storytelling, of bards and poetry, of Sacred story and song. That is the tradition in which I place myself as storyteller-poet-minister, and immersed within it I was pushed to improve and grow in painful and life-giving ways.

The University held a workshop for late-stage PhD students, and I was accepted into the program. It was three days examining the breadth of skills we had been developing as post-graduate students, in preparation for the task of finding occupations beyond the PhD. Sessions focused on leadership, research, team building and collaboration, and branding. Yes, we were guided through a process of reflecting on and naming our "brand". In the glut of "influencers" on social media in the years since my doctoral studies, this concept of a personal brand seems far less foreign than it did to me then.

Part One: Play

I had been living into a vocation and identity of storyteller-poet-minister for five or six years by now. That vocation, and the process of identifying and claiming it, I describe to you a little later. This branding exercise was a chance to consider it anew, and from a different point of view. The Rev Dr Storyteller-Poet-Minister: to whom would I be offering, marketing, *her*, in coming months? That question took a further year to work through, but in the meantime, I saw in the vocation an opportunity. What I could offer the church, now, as this uniquely branded storyteller-poet-minister was a bringing together of the three. I would create prayerful poems or poetic prayers (poet) for personal and community devotion (minister) that engage with the biblical stories (storyteller) we hear together each week. Pray the Story was born.

I created a new blog site on which I posted these prayer-poems, a new one each week. And for my Patreon supporters, a new bonus: they got a set of four prayer-poems in advance, which would help with worship planning for those in such roles. They also got a bonus exclusive prayer-poem that would be unavailable to the rest of the world until I published a book.

Pray the Story has grown in numbers of people engaging with it, and in its expression. I have a story eucharist with a number of variations, prayers for weddings and other occasions, and new (or re-worked) words for old hymn tunes. I have published two collections of the prayer-poems, each a full three-year cycle of the Revised Common Lectionary.[4] The RCL is a set of four readings for every Sunday (and extra festival and saints' days, too), which many churches use to help their communities hear from the breadth of the Bible across the years. I have crafted retreats that invite participants into the practice through which I create Pray the Story. In 2022, Pray the Story was relaunched as a subscription audio devotional / podcast, in another, short-lived, experiment to provide a source of income in an attempted season of freelance ministry as storyteller-poet-minister.

Praying as playing

As I have read others' thoughts and experiences with play, I have discovered how some have found links between play and prayer. Brian Edgar, for example, claims that "learning to play enables one to pray because it creates the capacity for exploring other worlds beyond the one immediately

---

4. *Pray the Story* and *Pray the Story Volume 2*.

present."[5] Apparently, Thomas Aquinas valued playfulness so much "he argued the one who does *not* play risks falling into sin."[6] "Both play and 'the contemplation of wisdom' [prayer] are undertaken purely for their own sake," Edgar notes, still following Aquinas, "with no other motive or function in mind, and both play and the contemplation of wisdom are done solely for pleasure."[7]

Pray the Story became, for me, a spiritual practice. A playful spiritual practice. Once a month, I took a day and engaged with the Sacred Story portions we would hear as a community in coming weeks. I wrote the dates and the four portions for each, by hand. I write most things by hand at first.

| 14 FEB | JOEL 2:1–2, 12–17 | PS 51:1–17 |
| ASH WED | 2 COR 5:20B–6:10 | MATT 6:1–6, 16–20 |

Each day on which we will gather. Lent is full—starting with Ash Wednesday, six Sundays, four days of Holy Week, Maundy Thursday, Good Friday, and sometimes I have also composed a lament for the Saturday.

I read all four portions for each day aloud; I listen; I feel. What grabs my attention this time around? I often listen from my specific context, which has been congregations in Adelaide, Edinburgh, and Canberra. Studying poetry, I have learned that specificity actually opens up potential for connection with a wider audience than generalizing. Poetry and paradox—they fit well together. Where do these words from our sacred inheritance meet our lived experience today, I ask as I listen.

Then I write. I write freely, hardly editing. I write what I am praying in response to the Story. I write in my voice, Australian, educated, and carefully aware of my privilege. I do try to use language perhaps less "poetic" and more broadly accessible in congregations of diversity in age and experience. There, I do temper what I write somewhat. Or, how I write it. I use my Australian voice intentionally because in my experience we have many resources available to the church for community and individual prayer from North America and the UK, and we Down Under need our voices to lead us in prayer as well. Although these prayer-poems are poetic,

---

5. Edgar, *God Who Plays*, 12.

6. Edgar, *God Who Plays*, 11.

7. Edgar, *God Who Plays*, 11: "for Aquinas, there is no surprise that Proverbs 8 describes the joy of the Eternal Wisdom present with God at the creation of the universe as a form of play."

they are prayers into which I intend to invite others, so I use more everyday language.

At different times, I have shared Pray the Story as writing only, or with audio accompaniment. After one three-year cycle of the Lectionary, I collated the prayer poems into a book. The bonus prayer each month for Patrons only, I now included for a wider audience.

In both Pray the Story collections, I also included some hymns. In Canberra, I began composing new words to familiar tunes—or adapting familiar hymn words to reflect our growth in ideas and language, while retaining something of the hymn's original meaning. For some, this is unwelcome. Understandably, there were folk who noted I had not at first got it right with attributions. We play, step out, and sometimes make mistakes. But there were also folk who thought my playing around with our inheritance was disrespectful, that I was something of an upstart. Well, Shakespeare was described thus, and his words live on 400 years later, so I suppose I could be in worse company. There were folk who, although they could not articulate it as such, felt I had disconnected them from the hymns, from the family they loved with whom they had sung these words for a lifetime. I appreciated these folk for showing me where I had erred in how I had introduced the new or adapted words to the community. One Sunday, one Advent, then, I took a moment early in the service to say something like,

> I have chosen some well-known hymns today. For some, we will sing the familiar words, knowing that they connect us with our past and our loved ones, and we may adapt internally as our language and ideas have changed over time. For others, we will sing new words, for those coming in from the outside of church, or younger, and finding old words incomprehensible or alienating them from worship. We are a community that welcomes each other, that cares deeply for each other. We do not want to alienate people in our singing, when singing involves our whole being. The words need to help us sing what we believe. So we need a balance: the familiar and loved to connect us to our ancestors; the updated and new to meet us where we are now, and welcome each other in.

One person in the front, who had until now refused to sing any of the new or adapted words I put before them, that day, from verse two of the first adapted hymn, began to sing.

Along with the hymn words, I also include in each *Pray the Story* book my "story eucharist" and its later iterations, such as for Christmas, or with expanded congregational responses. I had composed a simple liturgy for

Holy Communion for the Network of Biblical Storytellers' Australian gathering some years earlier. It had later been used in the international gathering, after which the blog post with the eucharist was the highest clicks I had ever had for a single post, four times the previous highest engagement. There are several versions of the story eucharist across the first and now second volume of *Pray the Story*, as I continue to play with it and adapt it for new seasons and moments. My hope is that others who use my prayers in community will also adapt them for their community. I am absolutely *not* comfortable with anyone doing that with any of my other writing. But with the prayers, they are invitation into prayer, which must meet those praying where they are.

I have taken my practice with Pray the Story and formed a retreat from it, to invite others into prayerful creativity: a retreat that invites participants to play and *thus* to pray. To hear the Sacred Story told from the heart, and to feel, imagine, respond with creativity. Most often, the invitation is to craft a prayer, as I have in my practice. Sometimes, with Psalms, I give people a structure to write a psalm of lament, for example, to play in the sorrowing space. Lament is something of a forgotten practice, yet it is vital to our being human. Lament reminds us that not only does being human include our brokenness—and lament allows us to name that brokenness healthily, with hope for healing—but also includes our embodiment, our imagination, our relationality.[8]

In my own act of playful response to painful circumstances, after I left my previous congregation without another to go to, I took the opportunity to experiment. I had previously played with my vocation as a freelance storyteller-poet-minister (again, I expand on that later). For now, this interim season seemed to present an opportunity to try again. I found much in the idea of freelance to be enticing. A certain freedom, the creativity and variety—*play*.

Pause

Listen to a Pray the Story prayer-poem or playlist on SoundCloud https://soundcloud.com/sarahtellsstories

---

8. Bargár, *Embodied Existence*, 147.

Part One: Play

Playing, praying—paying?

One thing I thought I would try was to monetize Pray the Story again. I thought this time, a subscription podcast, following encouraging signs of the numbers of people engaging with the blog from different countries and Christian traditions.

I tried building on a rule of prayer. To the playlist of new prayer poems for the week's lectionary portions, I would add

- Themed playlists—praying "justice", or "women", or "creation"
- A journal of practice—to accompany a themed playlist with invitations to create your own prayers or poems
- A daily office—prayers for dawn, noon, dusk, night, new for each season
- Playlists with prayer-poems from the books.

Subscribers got new content in text and audio, and a discount on the books in order to access the text for the older prayers.

Although a few faithful friends did subscribe, and added some financial support through a difficult year, even they did not regularly, or at all in the end, listen to the playlists I composed and compiled for them. I spent thousands of dollars setting it up in a season in which I had little to no income. Play is about taking risks, as I have explored with you already. And surely there were reasons such as the post-covid financial strain many were feeling and insufficient promotional activity. But ultimately, I saw that in this season, rather than playing I was floundering. I was hurting, to the extent of being utterly broken in my spirit. In some ways, having some ideas and projects to play with during this time did help, and perhaps I have again planted seeds for a future season. In the end, as I have since returned to a placement with a congregation and engaged in rebuilding my life, I have chosen to do so smaller. Part of the healing has been finding peace with failing, again; quite costly this time in terms of money, and yet, also liberating. This failure has helped me to let go of the freelance idea and more fully embrace a solitary life lived embedded in community as minister in placement with a congregation. Brené Brown says "if we are brave enough often enough, we will fall. Daring is not saying 'I'm willing to risk failure.' Daring is saying 'I know I will eventually fail, and I'm still *all in*.'" I've set out with courage in pursuit of dreams that have morphed into something I never imagined; dreams that caused me hurt in the striving to realize them; dreams I have had to leave behind for something that took me by surprise. I'm not sure I call all those scenarios "failures", but most of them feel like it at least for a time. And yet, even when I am broken, I have enough trust in the Source of my Life to say I know I will fall, and still, I am all in: I am here to play.

Invitation to reflect

Is play a posture you take in your various roles in life?

What gift/s does, or might, play offer you and your community?

What might be the cause of any reluctance you feel to adopting a posture of play more often?

Is there another posture you take, which my reflections on play brings to mind for you?

Do you have questions of my story or the ideas I have explored; of yourself and your story?

How will you explore your questions with curiosity? Journal, art, meditation, talking with others?

Part Two: Tell

Every human existence is a life in search of a story
Brian Edgar, *A God Who Plays*

Story

"To have a life is to have a story . . . many stories."[1] To have a story, or many stories, carries with it a responsibility to tell those stories, to share the wisdom of our experience to provide each other resources for living.[2] For Douglas Purnell, "stories are . . . a way of doing pastoral theology— the art and discipline of tending and attending to the lived experience of the people given to my care and holding that experience with the received church tradition in order to try to make sense of it, or at least to bear it."[3]

Importantly, in a culture that seeks to ignore pain, that privileges the telling of stories of happy, of success, the church's tradition of storytelling the breadth and depth of human experience is vitally countercultural. To sit with suffering "demands time, attention, courage, and endurance, and our culture supports denial of suffering;" although "distractions and posturing . . . may provide momentary relief, traces of anguish and ache linger on."[4] From the Christian counselling context, Nolasco asks, "what would the journey to healing look like if an attitude of compassionate acceptance and expansive presence pervade the counselling process?"[5]

With a curious, playful attitude to life, as we have seen, I have developed some capacity for the courage to be vulnerable, open to "failure." I seem to have grown into adulthood as John Cacioppo describes it, "not to become autonomous," or independent of others, but "to become the one on whom others can depend."[6]

I have always been a storyteller—I learned to read by learning the stories my parents read to me, then recognizing the words on the page. My teacher in Year 7 (then the final year of primary school) gave me a "writer's

---

1. Daniel Taylor, *Creating a Spiritual Legacy: How to Share Your Stories Values and Wisdom*. Grand Rapids, MI: Baker Publishing Group, 2011, xi.
2. Taylor, *Spiritual Legacy*, xi.
3. Purnell, *Being in Ministry*, 1.
4. Nolasco, *Contemplative Counselor*, 34.
5. Nolasco, *Contemplative Counselor*, 34.
6. Brené Brown cites Cacioppo in *Dare to Lead*, 25.

Part Two: Tell

folder", with pages of hints and tips for the emerging writer, such as "take a notebook and pencil everywhere." Mrs Bergin was the first person I remember naming the writer I was. As I have progressed through, first experiences of depression, then the call to ordained ministry, "leadership", and the practice of pastoral care, it has been the telling of story that has shown me how. Story's openness to truth that is multivalent, fluid, full of possibility for meaning-making and connection to self and others, and Divine. "Stories are, by their nature, dynamic, hybrid, and interactive. If they are to be living stories, the process of their formation is never completed."[7]

Profound reading for me around the time of The Esther Project, and for many in the mainstream protestant church, was *Christianity for the Rest of Us* by Diana Butler Bass.[8] In it, her chapter on "Testimony" reminds the reader of the way a person's being is nurtured when they feel heard. It is part of why "testimony", or telling our (faith) story has in many times and places been a rich and meaningful practice for church communities. Even more than this, for Daniel Taylor, telling our own stories is a responsibility of each of us to thus pass on what wisdom we have gained through experience.[9] For Megan McKenna, "storytelling is an art." But more than that, "it is basic to communication. Some say it is essential to our survival as human beings."[10] In many ways, stories keep us alive.

I learned I am one who can be—who *is*—trusted to hold the stories of our tradition, delve deeply into them in order to guide others into and out of them for *their* meaning-making discoveries. I have learned I am one who can be and is chosen with trust to hear others' stories, to hold them and their tellers safe as they are heard and thus nurtured towards their wholeness of being. For, held within God's story, a story of resurrection, renewal, transformation, as we retell our story, or re-story ourselves, we find healing.[11] In a vocation I came to name "storyteller-poet-minister", initially, storyteller was the dominant lens through which I learned to know who I was becoming. I have learned that story invites others to join with me.

---

7. Bargár, *Embodied Existence*, 17.

8. Diana Butler Bass. *Christianity for the Rest of Us: How the Neighborhood Church Is Transforming the Faith*. New York, NY: HarperCollins, 2009.

9. Taylor, *Spiritual Legacy*, xi.

10. Megan McKenna, *Keepers of the Story. Oral Traditions in Religion*. New York: Seabury, 2004, 195.

11. Bargár, *Embodied Existence*, 17.

Story

Story and identity are intricately interwoven, as Doug Purnell observes: "stories need to be remembered and retold, for they shape identity."[12] So to show you how I came to lead by story, I need to tell you the story of how I have come to understand my identity.

∽

Pause

What does the idea of story evoke for you? Thoughts, ideas, memories, feelings?

Is there a story that returns to you in different seasons, has accompanied you through your living, with a sense of comfort, belonging?

∽

---

12. Purnell, *Being in Ministry*, 146.

Discerning

Ordained

The Esther Project had been my placement for the Supervised Field Education component of formation for ordination. There's a lot of church jargon in that sentence, so let me explain!

The Uniting Church—as with Catholic, Anglican, Methodist, Presbyterian, and many other denominations—calls and sets apart an order of people to lead the church in Word and Sacrament and as Deacons. How Deacons serve in each of the traditions varies a LOT, but in the Uniting Church, Deacons and Ministers of the Word are both ordained for life, are equal, and differ in the nuance of their service. Deacons tend to be called to serve in the wider community; Ministers of the Word tend to be called to serve within the church. Both serve God, church, and wider community from their different locations.[1] I felt called to ordination as a Minister of the Word; to serve from within the church and among its gathered people.

When you discern that call, you test it with the church through work with a mentor, conversations with various councils, and an application to become a candidate for ordination.

While you are a candidate for ordination, you are considered to be in "formation" for ordination. You undertake university studies, which include biblical, historical, pastoral, and theological subjects along with practical subjects like Clinical Pastoral Education and Supervised Field Education. The practical subjects focus on certain skills the student needs to develop and nurture, in pastoral care provision and various other facets of our roles,

---

1. The Uniting Church in Australia has done a lot of reflecting together on these two ordained roles in our midst. If you are interested this is a good place to start: Rob Bos and Geoff Thompson (Eds), *Theology for Pilgrims. Selected Theological Documents of the Uniting Church in Australia*, Sydney: The Assembly of the Uniting Church in Australia, 2008.

from crafting sermons and liturgies, to administration, Christian education, and community engagement.

From the start, the church acknowledged that my call to ordination was to a way of being a Minister of the Word unlike what we had come to know. The Church was undergoing much change, and would need to undergo much more in coming years and decades, if it was to remain vital, thriving, alive in a broader community context vastly different from the established pattern and structure solidified through the 20th century. Which is why the church has experimented with forms of congregational life and worship—Fresh Expressions or alternative church projects like Black Wood Jazz and The Esther Project. When we were looking at a placement for my field education, usually undertaken in a congregation so you can learn the rhythms and elements of congregational life for which candidates are being formed, my teachers and I wondered if it might help "pioneer" leaders like me to undertake field education in "pioneer" or "fresh expressions" settings. There weren't many of those at the time, but I am a pioneer, or so they kept telling me, and I had this idea for a fresh expression of church I wanted to try, so perhaps we could make that my field education placement?

For the Field Education Placement, my priority had to be preparation for ordination, formation for taking on a particular role and place in the church, for the rest of my life. Minister of the Word is an eclectic job. In part, that is why I had felt it calling me—I am an eclectic person. I have empathy, performance acumen, language skills, musicality, scholarly curiosity, a contemplative posture, and commitment to community. In Minister of the Word, I felt the disparate gifts and passions that at one time splintered me in various directions, at last begin to coalesce, bring me into wholeness. Minister of the Word is also a role that demands a certain openness to the ongoing call of Holy One and the Church into different placements—congregations, chaplaincy, administration, teaching. All this was possible for my future, not only the type of fresh expression of church I started with The Esther Project. This meant in practice that my goals for the field education placement did conflict with the needs of The Esther Project.

As mentioned, The Esther Project was to be a theatre dinner show in Adelaide's 2016 Fringe Festival. When we met challenges, such as recruiting key personnel, the time constraints of the field education (a nine-month placement) meant taking the theatre show off the agenda all together, rather than simply postponing and having a longer lead time to build the community of creatives around the play. To focus on community gatherings without the added layer of a theatre event to prepare seemed the best way to meet the field education goals, although it meant compromising the initial goals of The Esther Project.

Those conflicts of purpose and priority formed one cause of the end of The Esther Project. I have discussed allies in part one; the lack of strong relationships with allies also contributed to our short life. Misunderstandings and miscommunications meant missed opportunities with our host congregation and the placements committee. There, my request for a part-time placement was heard, but not the attendant request for help (both financial and structural) to keep The Esther Project going alongside such a placement. That led to difficult years financially for me personally, only made less so by generous landlords, congregation, and friends who found me short term part-time gigs alongside my first congregational placement as a Minister of the Word.

I was ordained alongside four friends on 5 December 2010, and began at Belair Uniting Church in January 2011. Belair was five minutes down the road from Blackwood, the congregation which supported my candidature. I served there for three and a half years, the final years of the formation program. These were important years in the discerning of my vocation and identity as storyteller-poet-minister, the significant life that grew from those Esther Project seeds before the growth of the PhD years.

Storyteller

UNDERSTANDING MYSELF TO BE a storyteller had become the dominant lens for my self-reflection during the years of discerning, applying, and preparing for ordination. By "storyteller", I mean a practitioner of the art of oral storytelling: learning and telling stories by heart with a gathered audience, or in my case more often a congregation.

I also mean a holder of the stories of my community, to tell and interpret for our new times and experiences. One of my mentors along the way treasured the image of the breaker of bread to describe their self-understanding as a Minister of the Word. For me, it is storyteller: it is through seeing myself as a storyteller that I took my final step to accepting the call I was hearing to be a Minister of the Word.

I live out this element of storytelling through preaching, teaching, and scholarship, as much as through the inhabiting of biblical stories and telling them with the gathered people. The scholar in me was honored at college with encouragement to take all the Biblical studies opportunities; and later with the invitation to teach when the college had a shortage of available teachers. Before I had even studied Honors in biblical studies, and under the mentoring and supervision of others, I taught Biblical Hebrew and Prophets at undergraduate level. The college supported my accreditation as a VET assessor, and I wrote and taught certificate level subjects for lay preachers and leaders in the Vocational Education and Training stream at college.[1] I continued to assess in those VET subjects from Edinburgh, much of the way through the PhD years. Although in the years since the PhD, my primary scholarly community has been the Network of Biblical Storytellers' Scholars Seminar, I did return to Uniting College for Leadership and Theology as Adjunct Faculty teaching Biblical Studies for a couple of years on my return to Adelaide.

---

1. Vocational Education and Training courses are often delivered through the TAFE (Tertiary and Further Education) sector, which is similar to community college in the USA.

Part Two: Tell

Back when I was taking the Pastoral Care units of study during formation for ordination, I encountered a point of resistance within. It was the only real point of resistance in embracing the role of Minister, and I have struggled with it again at different times since ordination. Somehow, sometimes, I have not seen myself as someone to be relied upon in another's difficult moment. Then I prove my fears wrong again and again when I sit with a family and their dying loved one, welcome them to church, and his widow continues to participate long after her husband—the one who had felt the pull toward church—has died and I have conducted his funeral. Or I hear the stories of LGBTQI+ folk ostracized from Church and tell them in my words and actions they are welcome, they are loved, and not least by commissioning a new stole solely for the conducting of rainbow weddings. Or I hear stories of mental illness, and stay put, so that someone can, for once in their life, feel they are heard, are worthy, are loved.

In part, I found my way to this capacity for pastoral care through story. Our college offered us support in our formation for ordained ministry not only through their own programs, but by helping us gain training, education, experience beyond the college, beyond even the church. I had heard about Narrative Therapy, and wondered if these principles and practices might meet me in my strength, to address an area of lower confidence. In a one-week introductory course, I learnt about the application of curiosity and wonder in therapeutic (translated to my context of pastoral) conversations. I absorbed the language and approach of respecting the person before you as the author of, the expert in, their own story. Yes. *That* I could do. I could be, as a teller of stories, a *hearer* of stories. I understand story. Its power. Its possibility. I can sit beside you and hear your story, hold your story and you, safe. I would learn this of myself again in practice, as I have narrated in "Play", through the experience of facilitating gatherings for The Esther Project.

So I am a performance artist: a storyteller.
I am a scholar, preacher, and teacher: a storyteller.
I am a holder of stories Sacred and human: a storyteller.
I "lead", I offer accompaniment, through story.

Storyteller

Pause

What are you hearing?

How are you feeling?

Where is my story connecting with your story?

Story is mutual—on finding "enough"

Brené Brown writes:

> As a leader, I no longer check my personal life at the door. In fact, sharing stories and leading through the lens of multiple perspectives and experiences has made me more approachable and relatable to my students, staff, and community. By sharing my story and my *why* for leading, I helped my staff to understand my purpose, passion, and commitment to courage. It also gave others permission to practice vulnerability and to be brave in sharing and owning their life journey.[2]

I have mentioned mutuality a couple of times in passing as I shared of scholarship, of interpreting Esther and Romans through Play. Mutuality is core in my understanding of our humanity, of the Holy Dream for our wholeness and healing. I wrote in my PhD thesis that mutuality "has a quality of mutual obligation born of mutual need: of other-regard that seeks the good of the other first, *and also* good of self. . . . The give and take of relationships of true mutuality is intrinsically beneficial to both parties to the relationship."[3] Sharing our stories is inherently, profoundly, mutually beneficial. I have come to understand that what congregations look for from me as a minister is less to "lead" them, and more to accompany them, for, as Sue Pizor Yoder learns from Zelda, "It's dangerous to go alone."[4] Telling our stories brings us together, shows us our shared humanity. That I have

---

2. Brown, *Dare to Lead*, 179.

3. Agnew, *Embodied Performance*, 26 (emphasis original).

4. Sue Pizor Yoder and Co.Lab.Inq. *Hear Us Out. Six Questions on Belonging and Belief.* Minneapolis: Fortress, 2023, 17.

some courage for vulnerability and entering the hard stories gives me both the opportunity and the responsibility to be with my community in their stories, to facilitate their telling of their stories, and the embodying of the Sacred Story through their own. "There isn't a stronger connection between people than storytelling."[5]

During my first placement as an ordained minister, the storyteller part of my vocation was further clarified for me through a number of experiences.

In my first year, 2011, I was teaching biblical studies at the college from which I graduated that very year. I also attended my first Network of Biblical Storytellers' International (NBSI)[6] Festival Gathering, and learned about their Scholars' Seminar. I had been part of NBS Australia for a number of years, since my first gathering in Sydney. It was there, when on a walk with folk who are still friends today, that I had heard affirmation for me as a storyteller *and* as a potential minister-storyteller. "We need more artists in the order. We need more ministers like you." Waking up at home the first morning after that gathering, I knew I would apply to become a candidate for ordination: a minister, a storyteller. Since then, I had attended gatherings in Victoria and Queensland, and co-hosted a gathering in Adelaide.

NBSI began in the USA, and by far still the largest number of members call USA home. It has grown—for a time, a small but dedicated group held annual gatherings in Australia, as I mentioned, and overseas missions have sparked guilds in places like South Korea and India. Canada also has enough members to hold an annual gathering there, with many Canadians also attending the international gathering in the USA.

Friends from Australia have been going to the international gathering for years, and hearing their stories, I developed a desire to attend also. The Festival Gathering[7] moves every three years, and for my first, we were in the Blue Ridge Mountains outside Asheville, North Carolina. Ministers get two weeks' study leave each year, as we are expected to participate in ongoing education and professional development. I spent my first ever study leave at a Christian artists' retreat (more on that when we consider the "poet", anon), then at the NBSI Festival Gathering. I took a workshop in Bibliodrama, heard storytellers of differing experience, style, and ministry contexts, and participated in a masterclass. In this, I admit I was again

---

5. Yoder, *Hear Us Out*, 16, citing Jimmy Neil of the International Storytelling Center.
6. Network of Biblical Storytellers International: nbsint.org
7. Now known as the Annual Conference.

somewhat disappointed when, as in the first masterclass I had taken in Australia with a professional storyteller, I received the feedback, "there is nothing I can teach you. I would not suggest you do anything different." Now, I had no specific training in this artform. Sure, I've been on stages or before congregations all my life, and I understand story from the perspective of audience, composer, and performer. But no-one is perfect. Surely, there was *something* I could learn? However, after the initial disappointment, I settled into the gift of affirmation that feedback ultimately gave me, hearing I had within enough for this. Twice, from more experienced tellers, I had heard: "you are good at this."

Alongside my half-time placement, I had taken some short-term part-time jobs—filling in for a hospital chaplain, helping out in the Synod office. But I was trying to build up some freelance storytelling for that other "half time". It was a long hard slog. The church has historically assumed ministers will do stuff for nothing for the wider church, and the same goes for artists and volunteers with all kinds of expertise. I found it difficult to entice churches to pay me (at all, let alone appropriately) to lead retreats or workshops for them. Actually, it was a challenge to entice them even to have me along, regardless of the price: to consider I might have skills and expertise to help their people grow into their giftedness in particular areas. Oh, it was a challenge.

In a half-time placement, I worked full time through the liturgical high seasons of Lent and Advent/Christmas. This meant that I could take time in lieu in other seasons, to concentrate on the freelance ministry. I did so in late 2012, as a storyteller on tour in Western Australia for two weeks. I had received an invitation to be guest speaker at a church camp. I reached out to see if anyone else would like a visiting storyteller over that side of the country. A few people did take the opportunity and hired me for story workshops and preaching in Margaret River and Perth, along with that church camp.

Financially, I just about broke even. Personally and professionally, I grew. I gained insight into myself as a freelance "consultant." For example, I am not very good at the behind the scenes stuff a freelancer has to do. Promotion and book-keeping the main tasks with which I continue to struggle. I had not done well with these tasks as a freelance editor, either. The self-promotion, constantly touting for business, the setting of itineraries and travel details, managing money. If I could have a PA who made all the arrangements for me, so all I need to do is develop programs, learn stories, and turn up and hold people in creative and sacred spaces, that would be ideal. But I would have to be good—really good—so as to earn enough to pay two people. Oh, it is a challenge.

I mentioned in "Play" that on resigning from a placement in 2021 with no other placement to go to, I took the opportunity to explore the freelance ministry option. Again, I found a reluctance to hire in a consultant—was it a "creative" consultant, a "local" consultant, even a "female" consultant people did not value? I encountered reluctance to pay, and in post-pandemic financial hardship, a genuine lack of capacity to pay appropriately. The amount of time spent on promotion, quotes, administration, let alone the preparing and presenting of workshops and retreats—I did not gain enough income to cover all that time. Not if I wanted to live in my own home and without the stress of financial hardship. Not if I wanted to live the life of a contemplative creative, rather than of hustle and grind culture. The question of money again: how can I pay the rent and live into my authentic vocation and self and place in community?

Tricia Hersey tells her story of rest saving her life.[8] She tells of the grind culture, capitalism's drive to earn more, do more, be more, that actually leaves most of us merely grinding out an existence. For Hersey, an approach to life that privileges rest actually yields enough. It's a different kind of hard work—a discipline and a commitment to resist the dominant culture, to step out of capitalism's pull. I have long felt drawn to the fulness of my being as a creative woman of God, and every step, backwards as much as forwards, is taking me further into that realization of being.

I wonder if you feel it, too, the tension between living well and society's pull into "more"? John Dominic Crossan sees humanity's greatest prayer (for Christians, shaped as The Lord's Prayer) as a hope for, a call into, a realm of *enough*.[9] Not *merely* enough, so one is only just surviving; that is not actually enough. Hersey speaks as a Black American, and the experience of the struggle it can be to achieve that kind of enough. The cost is that there may be sufficient food and rent, but there is insufficient sleep, time with loved ones, rest, play, community, dreaming—there is not enough *life*. God's dream for enough, which Crossan hears through the prayer Jesus teaches, is the life in all its fulness, the abundance, that Jesus speaks of elsewhere.

---

8. Tricia Hersey, *Rest is Resistance*, London: Aster, 2022, 184.
9. John Dominic Crossan, *The Greatest Prayer*. New York: HarperCollins, 2010.

Let's qualify "abundance", too, while we're here: I don't mean having surplus to hoard. Such hoarding is borne of and elicits fear—fear that I won't have enough tomorrow, fear that keeps me from sharing with you in case I don't have enough later. Abundance is found in the Holy, in the Way of community into which Wisdom invites us. Together, in trust. When those who can, hoard the surplus, the abundance of resources becomes unavailable to others. This creates a false experience of scarcity, for there *is* enough, when we take sufficient for our needs and look to our neighbor to help them to meet their need.

The Old Testament / Hebrew Bible tells of the people of Holy One learning about "enough", with manna falling like dew from heaven each day. No matter how much the people took, more than what your tent needed, or less, all in every tent ate enough without anything left over. This was an invitation to remember their Holy One is trustworthy; that God is God and we are not. It is hard. Especially after traumatic experiences such as the slavery the people of God had experienced, and in the uncertainty of wandering through the desert without a secure home.

When I have been in seasons of limited finances, part-time work alongside study or writing, freelance self-employment, the pressure of rent and food and bills made it feel necessary to hustle to seek more work and income; to take on work more than I had time or capacity for, because I needed the money. It is a diminishing way to live. I found it demeaning to constantly "sell" myself. I found it demoralizing to be asked to justify my fees, my worth. I felt dejected often, when I was not hired, not paid properly, not, apparently, valued.

It may seem strange to say so now, but I am aware of the privilege I enjoy being able to choose in this current season to work part-time at one job. I have had to let go of the casual teaching work I had hoped could accompany my congregational placement, for the stress caused by carrying out responsibilities to two cohorts of people was causing me to suffer in physical and mental health.

For the first time in my adult life, when I lived in Canberra, I had been able to save for a house deposit. When I had to leave that position suddenly, without another to go to, those savings became a safety net to catch me in my brokenness. I could pay off the car loan to reduce the number of monthly debits. I sold the pool and paid that loan, too. I did not need to rush to find a placement before I was ready, as the savings invested in the freelance opportunities, and supplemented what small income I gleaned from contract and casual work over the next year. That was privilege; as was the gift of family who housed me and fed me for that first year of healing.

After a year I found a place to rent that is affordable, comfortable, secure, and located close enough to family and work. I live a fairly small life, keeping costs down somewhat. I can resist the grind culture pressures of status, success, more, obligation, and trust that the part-time stipend I receive is enough.

Enough that I do not stress about money.

Enough that I can even share with others less privileged.

Enough that I can choose joyful experiences that need paying for, from time to time.

However, I am aware that although I have enough now, I have lost the capacity to prepare for my future, now I am unable to work full time. This is scary, and it is a challenge to rest in trust.

Further, I am aware that although I have enough, it will not be completely enough until all are fed, housed, free, loved. All.

We are only fully human *together.*

Pause

Listen.

What is your "enough"?

How can our communities find courage and generosity to ensure "enough" for *all?*

Poet

DURING THE YEARS OF study for a Bachelor of Ministry and the formation for ordination, the poet was quiet. She made room for the academic and the storyteller, and gladly. But in that first minister's study leave period, my first stop was Santa Fe, New Mexico, for The Glen Artists' Retreat.[1] And there, I encouraged the poet to speak again.

I had found poetry as an angsty teenager, around the same time I discovered Shakespeare. Coincidence? I doubt it. My first poem—well, probably not, but certainly an early one—was written, age 16, on a school trip to New Caledonia, in French. "Le Rêve" (The Dream). I still remember the title. The rest of my poems have been in English, though French, German, Latin, and Scottish Gaelic have all made appearances.

I don't think I have told you yet how I love language, languages. At one time I thought I would like to be a translator, or write English subtitles for French films. I did not imagine I would, instead, write new translations of the Hebrew and Greek in the Bible for storytellers and scholars to play with in an international scholars' seminar for a network of biblical storytellers. And I do so with the poet front and center. The poetic nature of my translations is what makes them distinct, and adds to the richness of our discussions in the seminar. I do so love a scholarly forum in which my poetic gift is valued. Take a break and enjoy my translation of Micah 6:1–8.

---

1. Hosted by Image. imagejournal.org

Part Two: Tell

Scene One: Summons. *The Valley Court Room*

PROPHET Hear, I pray, what Breath of Life says:

Breath of Life Arise! Plead your case before the mountains;
let the hills hear your voice!

PROPHET Hear, Mountains and Perpetual Foundations of Earth,
the case of Breath of Life.
Breath of Life has a case against Their people,
and with Israel They will argue.

Breath of Life My people, what have I done to you?
How have I worn you down?
Answer me.

I have brought you up from the land of Egypt,
from the house of slaves
I redeemed you,
I sent before you Moses, Aaron, and Miriam!

My people, remember, I pray,
what Balak King of Moab instructed,
and how Balaam Son of Beor answered him
from Shittim to Gilgal:
remember, in order to know the just acts of Breath of Life!

Scene Two: Reply. *The Sanctuary*

HUMAN With what shall I meet Breath of Life?
Will I prostrate myself before Holy One on High?
Will I meet Breath of Life with sucklings,
with calves—young ones of a year?
Will Breath of Life be pleased with thousands of rams?
With overflowing torrents of oil?
Shall I give my first born for my transgression?
The fruit of my body for sin of my being?!

Pause

Poet

PROPHET/ PRIEST	They have declared to you, Human, what is good; what BREATH OF LIFE is seeking from you: Only— to do justice to love lovingkindness to make attentive your walk with your Holy One.

Through my first degree, in which I studied French, along with Legal Studies and Psychology, I wrote a lot of poetry. Of course, there were love poems: I had not yet settled into solitary as my way of being. I still bought into the narrative we are sold in my culture—many cultures I suspect—that all adults are incomplete until they have partnered, at least, if not also parented. That imprint on our DNA as with all species, the drive for the species to survive. But after many years living with Depression and learning to live well with it; after many years of self-reflection as part of the formation process, I eventually came to understand I was whole, and happy, single, and not parenting. I am very much a community person—and I am very, very, solitary. I prefer to live alone, though I do get lonely, and definitely do not like the managing a house alone part of it. But that's what food and grocery deliveries, and pool- and house-cleaners are for, so I discovered in a season of financial security and learning to live well with ME/Chronic Fatigue (it's not quite time to tell that story, but I will, in later pages).

But when I was writing poetry at first, many *were* love poems, and most of them to or about the one person I ever thought I could, or would, marry. Ah—you're intrigued, aren't you? Good. Go and read *On Wisdom's Wings*. Those poems are mostly in there, though he pops up again, like a ghost haunting my pen, in most of the collections.

I also wrote through the Depression, when I could. When the Depression is bad, I can't write at all. But when it is not *so* bad, I write it down, in journals or in poems. The Black Dog also appears through most of my collections; though it, like the love poems, has much space in particular in *On Wisdom's Wings*. That's my first collection, and while its contents span about a decade of poetry writing, *On Wisdom's Wings* was, as a collection, born in that workshop experience in Santa Fe.

To choose a number of poems. To have them read by other poets. To read them aloud with those poets, hear their sighs, explore their questions. And to offer that gift to each of them in turn. I believed in my collection, at last.

Part Two: Tell

To sit with three of the group, after we had walked into town from the college base for the retreat, stopping to admire the terra cotta and turquoise colors of the houses along the way; to sit in a *chocolaterie* and sip hot chocolates while we read poetry aloud. I *believed* I was a poet, at last.

I had been writing poetry for a decade. I had studied poetry at university, in a Creative Writing Honors degree. And I had participated in many readings and workshops since then. But here, in the southern USA desert, with new friends, I found the belief that had so far eluded me.

I wonder how much the process of discerning my call to ordained ministry, engaging in formation and all its self-reflection, the affirmation of ordination and induction into a placement—how much all that self-confidence building helped me circle back to the poetry and claim this, too, as who I am? I wonder how much the writing and collating of prayers for gathered worship week in and week out had helped exercise the poet muscles, so I could give voice to the poet again? In both cases, I suspect, a lot. As a poet, I am certainly also a liturgist. One who composes the words for the work of the people in worship.

After I had studied creative writing, and written those two plays for my church's Christmas Eve gatherings, I had explored the possibility of writing worship materials for *Seasons of the Spirit*. That was an international resource used in a range of denominations around the world. When I first met Susan, the Editor, she gave me the information about how to audition to become one of their writers. Looking at the audition materials, I thought, I don't know how to interpret the Bible so as to help communities of faith to do so. I wonder how I can learn to do that?

As I looked up our theological college's website (it was then known as Parkin-Wesley College), I found information on the Period of Discernment. Now, I had heard about this during my time as secretary for the Synod Children and Youth Ministry Unit. It is a period—usually about a year—of study and meeting with a mentor to (as the name suggests) discern. For those wishing to apply to candidate for ordination, this year of discernment is required. But anyone can do the program, and it is comprised of some set subjects and some tailored subjects to help you explore your questions. I did not think I wanted to be a Minister or a Deacon at that stage, but I did think I wanted to take some time to discern. The worship writing thing was one in a string of doors I had tried since finishing English and Creative Writing studies, others being in publishing, editing, and a PhD in English. As I told you in "Play", I was offered a place in an English PhD program, but no scholarship, and I wasn't moving all the way to Perth with that financial insecurity.

As you now know from the stories of the storyteller I have already shared, the result of that year of mentoring and studying preaching and ministry was applying to candidate as a Minister of the Word. None of my friends or family were surprised when I announced I was pursuing this direction, by the way, though it had me startled for a good few months! Several years later, as I drew the formation process to a close, and prepared to take on my first placement, I received an invitation to write the liturgy for a *Seasons of the Spirit* season. Full circle, from poet through storyteller back to poet, via Minister of the Word.[2]

Pause

Read or listen to some poetry for a moment: a different voice, a different way of using language.

---

2. I have circled back to *Seasons* a number of times since, writing for them during the intervening period after thesis submission and VIVA in Edinburgh, and in 2022, as part of the editorial team for the final instalment of its next iteration, *SeasonsFusion*.

Minister

THERE IS A MUCH older triplet than my three-fold naming of a vocation, used to describe the role of a minister—pastor-prophet-priest. Which is to say as *pastor* we have the responsibility of pastoring, or caring for, a community (congregation, school, hospital, presbytery). By care, we mean spiritual support through prayer and practice, presence in times of distress, and in joy; we mean education in the Christian story and tradition; we mean building and nurturing community. As a *prophet*, a minister is expected to proclaim the word of Holy One in word and action. As prophets have before us, we call the people's attention to injustice in the world with an invitation to raise their voices; to needs in the community with an invitation to turn up and offer kindness and compassion as they can. We remind our people of the Way of Love and call us back again and again, because we mis-step more often than we would like, or like to admit. A minister's *priestly* responsibility is to gather the people for the work of the people in worship. We baptize, we preside at Holy Communion (or The Eucharist). We help the people praise, confess, hear Holy grace, speak our gratitude, and bring our concerns to the Divine. We gather the people to send the people out into the world to be light, bring peace, show love, in our everyday living.

In my first placement, I was gifted with a small healthy congregation, used to having a half-time ministry placement and sharing the leadership and care of the people with the minister. They were, then, well established in rhythms of church life into which I was welcomed to find my place.

I shared *priestly* duties with retired ministers and lay leaders of wisdom, generosity, and creativity. I took the posture of setting the tone, with themes of focus for each season, careful structure of a roster of leaders and preachers, and in collaboration with a range of folk in the congregation for decorations, music, and the meaningful participation of all from youngest to oldest. Advent and Christmas seasons invited creative engagement with the characters of the stories, one year, through our youth, who were learning drawing technique with one of our adult members with angels as their subjects. They drew a series of angels which we then hung on purple fabric at the front of the church, to be joined by various types of angels brought in by other members to decorate the space. During that season, members were inspired to share with me of their encounters with angels, however they identified them as such, profound gifts rarely shared. Their stories, and angels as an important symbol, live with me still. Another year, the youth—and they invited other members to join them—created fabric statuettes of the characters in the Nativity scene. One of the older members made a stable and someone sourced some straw, and we built our own Nativity scene through the weeks of Advent. I crafted liturgies that responded to the creative ideas the youth leaders had, empowered and encouraged this leadership of the whole church by our younger folk, and brought my own creativity to partner with them.[1] We brought our creativity together on Christmas Eve to enact the story together. Others have purchased the script to use in their congregations, and I have used it with three further congregations.

One of our members was an artist, and his series of images representing Bible stories was displayed in the church for a time. I used photographs of his paintings, with permission, as the focus images on the screen I managed to convince them to install. And one of those paintings, of Mary and Elizabeth greeting one another, he apparently amended after hearing a sermon I preached! One Lent, we invited members to take a small canvas and respond to a story or theme or mood of Lent, and we hung the pictures as a focus for our reflections. Painting, stitching, felting, drawing. All were invited to contribute to the shaping of our space, the telling of the story, and to celebrate each others' contributions.

One of the retired ministers in the congregation was proactive with *pastoral* care, and he fell into a pattern of dropping into the church to see me and update me on who he had seen that week. That was a novelty for the congregation, actually, to have their minister work from their building. Before me, the ministers had been part-time here, and part-time down the road (at my sending congregation of Blackwood), and that church had a proper office set up, with administrator, photocopier, and more. I was *only* here. I set up a desk in the meeting room, and worked from the building two or three days each week to be pastoral, caring, with my presence. Which meant people could drop in to see me, or arrange to meet me there. It meant I had coffee most weeks with the folk mending bicycles in the men's shed, and was onsite for playgroup when that got started. It was an encouragement to the congregation to have their minister physically present in their

---

1. *Tell Me the Story of Christmas*: sarahagnew.com.au/shop.

home during the week, not only on Sunday mornings. I heard them say it felt I was more accessible, available, more "theirs".

A local choir shared that "home", rehearsing in the church hall. When one of their singers was coming to the end of his journey with cancer, he asked his wife to come with him to "his" church for worship, though they were not members of the congregation, and had not been part of "church" for many years. During those final weeks, the connection with a community of faith, and through them and their work together, with God, was a comfort I believe. That community continued to hold his wife after his death, and she became a collaborator with me in curating worship spaces with her floral art. Most memorable of these occasions was the first, when she created two beautiful purple-blue arrangements representing water for the baptism of an 8-year-old member. One of these we placed in the Chapel where the service began. The second was in the hall, to which the congregation relocated part way through, for the full-immersion baptism our young friend had requested. We borrowed a portable pool from a Baptist congregation a few suburbs away, and their water heater with it. I cannot forget, I am afraid, that the baptizee hit his head on the wooden structure as I tipped him back into the water! Apart from that slight mishap, a rich, meaningful, moment in which to participate as a community of faith.

Pastorally, the connections were indeed rich and profound: people inviting me into their vulnerable moments, the sacred moments of their lives. I performed the wedding of a music teacher who met her students in our building during the week. I chatted with our upper primary and secondary students in the kitchen over supper at a barn dance, about God and our doubts about where God is, even *if* God is, sometimes. And one of the most profound, of course, was towards the end of another life. I took communion to a member who was dying, our artist and former minister of that congregation; after I had told him of the people who had gathered, and the story we had heard, he put his hand on mine, looked into my eyes, ready for the Holy Meal, and said, *feed me.*

Prayer for a friend who is dying

(or perhaps a prayer for me as a friend is dying)

God who knows us more intimately
than we know ourselves,

my friend is approaching the transition
from this life
        to what comes next,
from known
        to unknown.

Be for him a source of comfort
and courage; be for him
the peace he seeks:

peace that he has lived into
the fulness of his being
with love and honor for you,
and others, and himself;

peace with his mistakes,
the mistakes of others—peace
that he has forgiven and been forgiven;

a peace that even as I pray
I do not understand for what I
am asking –

but we trust

we trust you

in this moment of need, we
trust that you are here
you are here

you are here

you are.[2]

The key act I recall when I look for the *prophetic* element of ministry for me during that first placement was shaving my head. It was Lent. My fourth year with the congregation. I felt for myself I wanted to embody the letting go of something I valued in this fasting season. In other years, I'd done chocolate; I'd done alcohol. I wanted something more.

    I had been spending hundreds of dollars on haircuts and colors of varying degrees of eccentricity, every five or six weeks, for years. Even when a poor student. Even now, a half-time minister. It was an embodied

---

2. Sarah Agnew, "Prayer for a friend who is dying", *On Wisdom's Wings*, 172. For Tony.

expression of a part of my identity. The crazy one. The eccentric one. The performer. But I had started to ask questions of myself, of this practice.

First. The money. Was this the most faithful stewardship of my resources? I was growing dissatisfied with the choice to spend money in this way, on appearance. Sure, I could rationalize it with the argument of enjoying life and living to the full and that being biblical. I could also argue for the artistry, for the self-expression, except that these defenses were not cutting it (hah!) any more. What it boiled down to was:

Second. Vanity. How much had I let my identity become tied up in my appearance? And was that where I wanted it to be? I did not. I was ill at ease with what my hair had come to mean for me, the need to be seen as eccentric, the need to be *seen* full stop. I wanted my identity to be centered within; with the depth of me, with the Sacred spark in me. I was claiming my *identity* as much as my *vocation* with "storyteller-poet-minister" over these past three years. And I needed to let old identity markers go. I needed to let go of practices no longer aligning with my vocation, my identity, the story I wanted to tell with my living.

I chose for my own Lenten practice to let go of my hair-dying and crazy cuts. I shaved it off, a number one all over. Then I chose to donate what money I would have spent on haircuts during Lent—the timing would have meant two visits to the hairdresser. I donated it to the Biggest Morning Tea, an annual event to raise money for Australia's Cancer Council, and attended the event being held by one of our congregation members in order to do so.

Why cancer? Well, the association with hair, and the hair loss many experience as a result of the treatments for cancer. For our congregation had gone through a rough season with cancer in recent times: members living and dying with it, their friends and family members living and dying with it, so that not one of us was untouched by its closeness, its grief.

Not only was shaving my head a re-set for *me*, asking can I be me without the crazy hair, and can I steward my resources with a deeper alignment to my values? This was also an act of solidarity with my congregation. It was a prophetic act. By donating the money I would save by *not* dying my hair through Lent to the Cancer Council I was saying *I see you. I am with you.* My people who are living and dying with cancer; whose family and friends are living and dying with cancer.

I see you.

I am with you.

When you look at my shaved head, see *our* grief, *our* pain, *our* loss.

I "lead", I offer accompaniment, when I enact our story.

I discovered that it was not the act alone that was prophetic. It was how I spoke of it, how I named the *why* of it. It was that I embodied the mutuality I preached week in and week out: my refrain "we are fully human only together" now visible in my standing in solidarity with my people in their, in our, pain.[3] I wrote blog posts reflecting on the impact of the shaved head on me: "one way to help people understand how much you care is to share your story."[4] How I looked in the mirror and did not know myself. How the loss exacerbated the Depression for a few weeks. How my experience opened my imagination and empathy for those who really *lost* their hair. How, surprisingly, I gained empathy for bald men, and they talked to me about their grief as we shared the experience of cold heads in the unfolding winter. I found that the prophetic act also opened up pastoral connections, and deepened my relationships with many members over my last months of a fourth year I would not complete with that congregation.

Pause

Ponder: it is hard to speak of being prophetic, being a prophet. It feels like it should be others who name it. And yet, I have claimed it, even embrace the symbolic element of my role.

Why are we scared to name the prophetic in ourselves? Do we even name it in others, with gratitude and celebration?

How are you feeling about prophets and prophetic words and actions? In your life, in those around you, in the Church?

---

3. I may have picked up the refrain along the way from reading or listening to Archbishop Desmond Tutu—he is known to have held this to be true.

4. Brown, *Dare to Lead*, 179.

Discovery: identity and vocation

IN 2013, THE YEAR before this prophetic act of shaving my head, I had taken another symbolic action: my first tattoo. I had been planning it for years; had a friend design it some time before. And now, with my understanding of my vocation and identity clearly becoming "storyteller-poet-minister", it felt wrong *not* to have the symbol of that identity on my person.

A quill is the kind of pen with which Shakespeare and Austen wrote. These two are important for me as writers, for different reasons. William Shakespeare is dramatist, performer, poet, storyteller, with imagination and empathy so deep as to evoke profound insight into human being. As I mentioned in "Play", I tell the story of my love for Shakespeare in the album *In His House,* and especially the title track.[1] Jane Austen gave me courage to stay single, as I grew in understanding, not so much of her stories, but of *her* story. Her motivations might have been very different to mine, her options, her sense of peace with it (or not). But, in a time when it was difficult to be a single woman, she was. In a time when women found it difficult to get published, she was. In a time and social context when it was perhaps unseemly for women to have an occupation, she wrote, and she earned money from her work. Nevertheless, the stories Austen wrote are part of the fabric woven around me that mapped the expected path for a woman: marry and raise children. While I grew up expecting I would have a career of my own choosing, and that I would do a PhD, I also grew up expecting I would get married. I didn't question that. I grew up expecting I would be a mother. I didn't question it.

Whether it was the experiences of Depression, which began at university, aged 17, and caused me to retreat deep within; or an innate part of my being I did not understand until well into my 20s, or even 30s, I cannot tell you. What I can say is that in my 20s I received a diagnosis of Polycystic Ovary Syndrome (PCOS). I first grieved a likely loss of motherhood as a consequence of this condition. Then, I grew to recognize my relief. By the time I could name my three-fold vocation, I embraced my non-parenting

---

1. Find *In His House* on the webshop: sarahagnew.com.au/shop, or bandcamp.

path as a choice. My creativity, generation, birthing, would be expressed in other ways in part *because* I wouldn't have children.[2]

I do think there is an element of Depression-induced consequences here. My energy is depleted. More so since I also have ME/Chronic Fatigue Syndrome. I find it takes energy enough to keep *me* alive and well that I cannot fathom keeping a small human alive and growing too.

I live in an interior world, and perhaps that is innate character. I feel almost ill at the thought of someone depending on me the way a child depends on an adult. For that matter, the way a partner depends on you; and you on them.

Through formation for ordination I grew to understand my energy as needing a balance of time with people and time in solitude. I am always learning how to draw on the gift of this balance for myself and for the communities in which I live and serve. And I will return to this later, too.

I choose to be single and childless because that is how I thrive. And in my thriving I contribute to the thriving of community. We are fully human only *together*.

Symbol and sign

By my 35th birthday, early 2013, I was clear with the vocation and identity into which I would grow and flourish for years to come. I had long wanted a tattoo—the hippy in me my mum cherishes. Some time ago I had asked a dear friend to design a tattoo for me: a quill, my chosen symbol for the writer, the storyteller, the poet. During the period of discernment, my mentor had introduced me to a series of books set in Ancient Ireland, with the Celtic bards and druids.[3] In these stories, the bards and druids carry symbols on their person of their role, their identity, their place in the community. From cloaks, staffs, and the instruments of their vocation—often a harp—to the way they cut their hair, a druid or bard was instantly recognizable to their people as such. Not for status or power. But, yes, for authority. For respect. For a reminder of the role and function of these people in, for, and *with* the community. Important, because druids and bards were wanderers, spending seasons in each community and moving on. So as a visitor, they were known to be of the order that were set apart to serve the

---

2. Here, I recall my poem "I am not a mother", *Whisper on My Palm*, 61.

3. Caiseal Mór. *The Circle and the Cross. Book 1: The Wanderers*. Melbourne: Random House, 1996. *Book 2: The Song of the Earth. Book 3: The Water of Life.*

people in this particular way, and an easy trust could be invested in them for their place in that order, in their culture.

Of course, as in any age, a minority behaving without integrity have tainted the symbols of my own order, and the trust they once invited is done for many. This deeply saddens me, and it is another story, not mine to tell. But at our best, that is what we clergy today are doing with our collars, Albs, and stoles. We are wearing the symbols of our order and place in the community, so the people can see who we are and, ideally, trust the role and the person. Perhaps I can take a moment to describe what these garments are, for those not familiar with the tradition. A reminder that my tradition is Uniting Church in Australia, protestant, with heritage in Presbyterian, Congregational and Methodist churches.[4]

The Alb—from latin *alba*, meaning white—represents our baptism, all the members of the body of Christ, baptized into the one Spirit. Technically, anyone who is baptized can wear an Alb, and I believe in some traditions or congregations, whoever is leading worship or reading from the Sacred Book will wear an Alb. My Alb has a collar, one pocket and one slit at pocket level, and goes on and comes off over the head. So, when I stepped into the minister role on the day of my sister's wedding, for which I was bridesmaid for most of the day, I needed help from an aunt and my mum to get into and out of the Alb without messing up the nice hairdo for bridesmaid's duties! In recent placements, where regular worship gatherings have a more informal feeling to them, I have worn an "informal Alb"—a long white dress—with the stole. These are also much cooler, a welcome option in our Australian summer. I wear a cross, too, the universal symbol of the self-giving love of God in Jesus. The cross I wear is one of eight made by a friend of mine, given to me on my 21st birthday. It is the basis of the design for the cross that features on my red stole. The stole is a scarf with a particular cut at the neck, worn only by ordained ministers. (There is another scarf, named as such, with a different cut, that can be worn by lay members: you'll see moderators or presidents wearing it if they are not ordained). The stole represents the yoke of Christ ordained ministers are understood to wear—that we step into the ministry of Jesus, a ministry of reconciling and radical love. Deacons in the Uniting Church wear a cross-body stole in a nuanced representation of the servant nature of Christ, again, into whose ministry

---

4. Discover more through the Assembly of the Uniting Church in Australia: uniting.church/about/. Specifically, you can search the Assembly website for more of the Uniting Church's policy on liturgical dress here: ucaassembly.recollect.net.au.

they too live. Clergy may wear stoles in colors according to the seasons of the church year. I have designed most of my stoles; they all feature symbols as well as the liturgical colors. The colors are Purple for Lent (more of a red-purple) and Advent (a blue-purple, or even blue), White / Gold for Christmas, Epiphany and Easter (also for sacraments of Holy Communion and Baptism), Red for Pentecost, Palm Sunday and other celebrations (like ordination and installation services), Green for Ordinary Time, which is a season between Epiphany and Lent, and a longer one after Pentecost. I also have a black one for Good Friday, and a rainbow one for presiding at rituals for LGBTQI+ folk. On my white stole, my mum embroidered symbols in gold—wheat and grapes for communion, a shell with water drops for baptism, and a Celtic cross. She made a matching lectern fall, and cursed the metallic gold thread throughout, an odd kind of blessing imbued therein! On the purple ones I have beaded candles (designed and embroidered by my mum's dear friend Gwen), unlit for Lent because we extinguish candles during Holy Week in preparation for the death of Christ, and lit for Advent because it is a season of preparing for the coming light of Christ. I also have a blue Advent one with angels, messengers from God. This one is a gift from supervisor, mentor, and friend, Sandy. I have two green stoles, one a gift from mentor, Anna, with wheat and grapes; the other made by my Auntie Chris has a Celtic tree of life and butterflies.

The black Good Friday stole has a cross and nails in silver, made by my mum.

The rainbow one is designed to look like rainbow paint running down a white stole. Again, I designed it, but it was sewn by Kirsty, who was a young adult in my first congregation and is now, as are her parents and sister, a dear friend. Kirsty did well with my crazy idea of paint dripping!

And the red stole. This one mum and I designed for my ordination, and it tells the biblical story from Genesis to the early church. It features the shape of the dove's wings from the Uniting Church logo, threads and materials from grandmothers, artwork from friends and stitching of sisters. My Mum made this one, and the white and black ones, and also helped with the stitching of the purple ones.

Liturgical garments help point through me to God. The role of our ordained ministers is, in part, to point to the life of Christian spirituality all members of the body of Christ have chosen to follow.[5] This is not a call

---

5. For more, see Sarah Agnew, "A presence assumed." For Act2 Theological Culture Papers, Produced by Uniting Church Assembly, 11 Oct 2023. https://act2uca.com/

to be perfect, or to be better than or above the non-ordained members of the church. Ours is not a call, as my friend Jo said to me, to be a moral authority, as much as it is to be "a source of comfort in difficult times."[6] It is a call to a particular role, immersed in the Sacred Story, entrusted with care of the members, asked to preside at the community's rituals with and on behalf of us all. We set aside some members for these tasks in order to do our best to ensure these central tasks of the community of faith are undertaken with care, respect, and integrity. The central tasks of the community, mutual love and care, immersion in the story, remembering through enactment of the story in baptism and communion are tasks for all in the community and for the community as a whole together. Members of the faith community are called to different vocations, within and beyond the church. Therefore, we need an order who are committed to the community of faith, to the church, for its health, and for the health of all followers of Christ, so that when we gather we perform our core tasks faithfully, and we are nurtured, equipped, and encouraged for our going out into the world. When I stand among a gathering of a Christian community as presider (preacher, worship leader, presider of baptism and communion), I stand as me, but not primarily as myself. The light of Holy One shines through me, picking up my particular colors—my personality, gifts, story—but that light does not stop at me. It flows from and to the Divine. I wear the white of our baptism, the cross of radical love, and the stoles of season, symbol, and story in order to remind me, remind us all, to look *through* me, listen through my words, to the Divine. It reminds us to look through the colors of each of us for the light of Holy One. It reminds each of us to nurture that light, those colors, in ourselves, so as to carry that radical, reconciling love in our own words and actions, wherever we go. I do not wear the liturgical garments to be looked at. In fact, I wear them precisely not to be looked at, my clothes speaking, as they do, and probably saying something I don't want to be saying in that moment. As an aside, those who refuse to wear liturgical garments, I ask you, do you really prefer the symbolic language of necktie pointing to masculine "power" down below? Or if you wear a dress, how long will it be, how patterned, how distracting? Historically and still today, women in particular are doomed whatever we wear. Clergy: we are set aside for a particular role in the community, and in that moment we

---

theological-culture/a-presence-assumed/.

6. Jo Schoenwolf, personal communication, December 2024. Jo co-hosts the podcast *What the Hell is a Pastor?*

are not one of the crowd. We must do whatever we can to fulfil our role, with its symbolic nature, and point beyond ourself to Holy One.

The clerical collar is that white strip in a shirt you will most often recognize as the garb of Catholic and Anglican priests. The collar for me is for the occasions when it is helpful for the people to be able to quickly recognize me as minister and I'm not wearing Alb or stole. Not because I'm special, or more important—it's not about status. It is, again, about symbol, and I embrace the symbolic nature of my role in Christian community. Ecumenically, the collar is a universal symbol of ordination. People could look across the room and know my place in the room, the community. Ministers' symbolic role is to be a reminder to the community of the call of God on all our lives. When Ministers preside at communion or baptize members (and in the Uniting Church, it is mainly ministers who can), we do so *with* and *on behalf of* the community. When I turn up at an ecumenical prayer gathering, I do so with and on behalf of my community.

I began wearing the collar more in my role as Rise Chaplain (I told you a bit about my connection with Rise earlier). Holding relationships with Rise also as a creative artist and collaborative partner, it was helpful for me, if not anyone else, to have a symbolic pointer to my role as Chaplain when I was engaging in events and relationships as such. It is a visible sign of the church, present in that setting, in the relationships we were building with women on the edges of and beyond the church community. I also hope that as a younger, female, tattooed, eccentric, progressive minister, I might upset some of the clichés and outdated images of who is and can be a Minister of the Church. This itself might invite new or renewed connections with Christian story and spirituality for those seeking a way of hope, while also conveying some sign that I am qualified to speak in certain settings.[7]

And I was telling you about that other symbol, my (first) tattoo, and why. I have told you of my role models and inspirations, Shakespeare and Austen. I have told you of the bards and druids and their symbols. I have told you of the symbolic garments clergy wear, and why I choose to do so. I appreciate symbol. For me, wearing the quill on my skin, by the hand with which I write and baptize and bless is a reminder to me of the place I have

---

7. A conversation on Facebook (20 September 2021) with friends Nicole Mugford and James Ellis helped with the clarification and articulation of these thoughts: thank you friends.

found from which to do what is mine in my community. A reminder for me, and those I meet.

I got it at a time when I was regretting not having it, so I was pretty sure I could live happily with this permanent ink. And I got it after I submitted three pieces of work:

- the manuscript for *On Wisdom's Wings*, my first poetry collection, about which I have told you;
- a proposal for TedXAdelaide, storytelling about storytelling, and using a story of faith in a secular setting, which told me I was a storyteller with and from my Christian tribe, for more than only that tribe; and
- an abstract for a scholarly conference on narrative, again using stories of faith in a broader setting, this time claiming a place in the scholarly community, while I was in the midst of Honors exploring narrative and performance in the book of Esther.

The important aspect of this timing of the tattoo, and why I belabor the story here somewhat, is this. I did not wait until these submissions were *accepted* before I claimed the symbol of my vocation to imprint on my skin. This was not a response to external validation, which would make it flimsy and suspect to threat of withdrawal. This was internal self-acceptance and celebration. This was the practice of courage, compassion, and connection that Brené Brown has identified as essential traits of those who live wholehearted lives.[8] Any community acceptance (connection) was part of that airing of my vocation (courage) without the need for those pieces of *work* to be accepted (compassion).[9]

---

8. Brown, *Gifts of Imperfection*. Chapter 1 in particular explores courage, compassion, and connection.

9. Interestingly, as well as *On Wisdom's Wings*, the other two submissions were also accepted in a year of profound growth and development as a storyteller-poet-minister. You can still watch the TedX talk here: youtu.be/OCAqvcqNE5g?si=QwO0W2HenrJ3psNF. My presentation to the narrative conference became a chapter in the book, sadly now out of print: "Choice: Story. Reception Theory and Storytelling: Choosing Stories to Tell and Ways to Tell Them." In Lena Moller, Minerva Ahumada and Laurinda Brown (Eds) *Perspectives in Storytelling. Framing Global and Personal Identities*, Oxford: Inter-Disciplinary Press, 2014.

Pause

Listen. Who are you becoming?

How do you affirm your identity in sign, symbol, action?

Scholar

AGAIN, I ALWAYS ASSUMED I would do a PhD. Possibly because Dad worked in the office of graduate research and scholarships at Flinders University all my younger life, and welcomed those PhD students into our home regularly. Far from home, often here alone or sometimes with a spouse, these students found welcome and friendship with my Dad and his family. PhD students, academics, published writers—all these were our inner circle throughout my growing up.

The University itself was a familiar place. The Registry building, where Dad worked, the lake, the pool at the lower campus where we went swimming in summer, the pine forest where we collected cones for the open fire at home, and the Alan Mitchell Sports Centre named for my grandfather, Mum's Dad, my Dad's mentor, founder of the Student and Sports Associations at this University in its beginnings in the mid 1970s. I did gymnastics in that center as a kid, believed his spirit was with me doing exams there in the '90s, and took photos beneath his name after walking across the stage inside, in my graduation gowns (borrowed, twice with their BA hoods, from mum and dad on different occasions). Much later, the Alumni magazine did a feature on our family after my middle sister graduated from Flinders with a PhD. This meant that all five of us, mum, dad, their three daughters, had graduated from and been employed by Flinders University—something we are fairly certain no other family can claim.

The path to my own PhD wound around a fair bit; inevitably, I will recap some of the story I have told you so far. After high school, I started a BA, planning to become a child psychologist working in Family Courts. After two years, I decided I wanted to be a writer, and changed from Psychology to French as a major alongside Legal Studies, just to get the degree finished. A clue to my writerly instincts may be found in my elective choices for Legal Studies, with "Media Law", and "Language, Literature, and the Law"; in the latter I got to spend time with Dickens (*Bleak House*), the Bible (*Job*), and Shakespeare (*King Lear*).

While I finished the French major part time, I worked in the Synod office. When on the front reception for a year, and needing to send an office-wide email to check the network function each morning, I often sent around a poem I had composed! The audacity of a 20-year-old! The poet, flexing her muscles.

After a year of full-time work, and being graduated for the first time, I decided to return to Uni to study English with a view to doing a PhD. I was granted permission to take second- and third-year subjects concurrent with first year—rather than after, which was the usual practice—and took seven subjects in one year. The next year, I enrolled in Honors (Creative Writing), with a thesis exploring the experience of depression as expressed in poetry.[1] The thesis was comprised of a creative piece, a collection of poetry I composed, and an exegesis engaging with Dorothy Porter's *What a Piece of Work,* Geoff Page's *The Scarring,* and the collected works of Philip Hodgins.[2]

I graduated again, and worked for a time as a freelance editor, mostly for a one-man publisher who became a treasured mentor for a number of years.

Eventually, I applied for a PhD and my thesis proposal was accepted by the University of Western Australia. I planned to explore the identity of William Shakespeare in Australia: who has he been to us here? But I missed out on a full scholarship, and was not prepared to travel all the way to Perth without it. A sign perhaps that this was not the path into thriving for me. Or that I was still young, still learning how to live well with Depression, and had not yet learnt to trust my own strength and resilience.

Fast forward to 2011 (about ten years), and I had completed a Bachelor of Ministry with a heavy load of Biblical Studies subjects. My lecturers identified both my aptitude for languages and for analyzing literature, and offered me much encouragement to continue in this area. I was invited to teach before I had barely graduated again, and had not yet even enrolled in Honors in Biblical Studies. I felt this to be another affirmation of my ability and the path my mentors were encouraging me along.

---

1. Sarah Agnew, "Love's Labors Lost. The Experience of Depression in Contemporary Australian Poetry," Flinders University, 2001.

2. Dorothy Porter. *What a Piece of Work.* (Picador, 1999); Geoff Page. *The Scarring.* (Hale & Iremonger, 1999); Philip Hodgins. *New Selected Poems.* (Duffy & Snellgrove, 2000).

Part Two: Tell

I had been toying with a number of possible projects for a PhD, and eventually settled on Biblical Performance, and the question I posed of Biblical Performance Criticism: where is the method for interpreting the Bible *by* performance? I have told you some of it, and *Embodied Performance. Mutuality, Embrace, and the Letter to Rome* tells that story in its fulness.[3] Now, though, I need to finally introduce you more fully to my storytelling tribe and main scholarly community.

Network of Biblical Storytellers

I briefly mentioned that in 2007 I attended my first Network of Biblical Storytellers gathering, on the outskirts of Sydney. My Aunty Chris had been a biblical storyteller, following the Network practice for some years, so I had heard about it. I would not say I thought of myself as a biblical storyteller in that way when I started telling biblical stories for our alternative church experiment, Black Wood Jazz, either by heart, reimagined, or reading aloud with dramatic intent and expression. I had not brought my knowledge of "biblical storytelling" together with my own intuitive approach, until my mum and I went to this annual gathering, sat in an introduction to biblical storytelling workshop with network founder Tom Boomershine and Amelia Boomershine, and I realized—this is me! This is what I do. This is *who I am*.

Later that weekend, as I have mentioned, on a walk with experienced tellers and ministry agents in diverse settings and traditions, I expressed my sense of wonder and self-discovery or identification perhaps. We were getting to know each other—in several cases, the beginnings of lasting friendships—and I was sharing my progress in the period of discernment. By this time, I had played with the idea of Deacon, and was now considering Minister of the Word. The Introduction to Preaching course, the connecting with others being called "pioneer", and now, storyteller. Rather than Deacon in the community beyond church, I knew I was to be present within. To change church practice from within. To change ordained ministry by being a Minister of the Word unlike Ministers I'd known before. I had a gift and a calling to be a holder of the story of my people, as the bards did of old, and to hear the story anew, our stories woven through it, and help the people live and tell the Sacred Story, our stories, well.

3. Agnew, *Embodied Performance*.

SCHOLAR

I returned to Adelaide from that first NBS gathering, and when I woke the next morning, I knew with all my being that my next step was to apply to candidate as a Minister of the Word.

The Network has been one of my most important communities ever since.

The Network of Biblical Storytellers has as its mission "to encourage everyone to learn and tell biblical stories."[4] The method we practice is to internalize portions of the Bible, from a few verses to whole books, in a translation accepted by the community (most often NRSV, more often now also CEB), or sometimes our own, and tell it by heart. Not "by memory", lest we make the mistake of thinking memory or storytelling is a head-only exercise. Although understanding is growing again of the embodied nature of memory and knowing (I write on some of that developing understanding in *Embodied Performance*).[5] We aim for 75% accuracy with the words we learn, and 95% accuracy with the story—get the plot, action, characters, dialogue in the right places at the right moments.

Naturally, there are folk who connect with the Network who do other things with story, with biblical story. At the annual conferences (formerly called Festival Gatherings, FG) we have a time of "lighting the fire" (though it is rarely around an actual fire, as we meet in summer), when we share the other stories we are learning and telling. I have shared poetic stories, one or two from my (in)humanity series, over the years. And people do play with biblical stories: I have heard some imaginative retellings, one Australian teller who did amazing things with accents for the Divine and angels, one or both of which were Scottish (of course). Some of our members also practice the Godly Play method of storytelling, though there's not actually a lot of overlap with practitioners of the two storytelling forms. The main difference I see in the methods is that with Godly Play, the teller's eyes are directed at the props during the telling, to direct the listeners' eyes there also. In biblical storytelling, the storyteller meets the listeners in the eye— and this is one of the main reasons I love it as a practice. The telling of our inherited stories for the people, meeting them in the eye. And if the eyes are windows to the heart, and I have internalized the story into my being, then I am telling these Sacred stories from my heart to yours. And thus, we can meet each other in the story, and meet and be met there by the Sacred.

---

4. nbsint.org
5. Agnew, *Embodied Performance*. See Chapter 4, particularly.

Part Two: Tell

The first time I attended the International FG, as I've mentioned, was in Asheville, North Carolina. I also told you that the week before that, I'd been in Santa Fe, New Mexico for The Glen Artists' retreat. From high desert to the high Black Mountain, and Black Bears were spotted on both sites while I was there, though not by me. One memory that stands out when I think of this first gathering is sitting in the dining hall with Richard Swanson, talking about my early thoughts for postgraduate study. It's well over ten years ago now, and although the feeling of affirmation and encouragement is as strong in my embodied remembering as ever, I cannot remember much detail of what we actually said. I may have expressed interest in Biblical Performance Criticism, and perhaps some frustration that I had not found a clear method there for the process of interpreting the Bible through this practice of internalizing and telling the Bible by heart. Richard was as I have come to know he generally is: curious, delighted by ideas and wondering and possibility. I came away from our conversation with the sense that I had been encouraged to go for it and write what I wanted to read!

That was 2011. That year, I taught biblical studies subjects at Uniting College. The next, I enrolled part-time in Honors. My project would be a study of Esther 4, the scenes in which Mordecai approaches Esther as the one ideally situated to petition the king for the protection of her people. I read this through a narrative lens, also posing questions from and for performance by oral storytelling. I may not have completed the play I had begun, nor staged the performance I thought would gather a community with The Esther Project, but I did return to that story and play with it some more.

When, in 2014, I began the doctoral studies I had been planning for some years, I contacted Phil, the convenor of the NBS Scholars Seminar. I knew some of my fellow Aussie NBS folk had connected with the seminar in various ways, and Richard had told me a little about it in 2011. Phil was as encouraging and welcoming as Richard, and I attended my first seminar, and second International Festival Gathering, in Maryland in 2015. I don't get very "fan-girl" about people who are famous or well-known. I try to respect people as humans of dignity and worth, whatever your achievements or status. I will confess, however, to a feeling of the surreal, when Joanna Dewey, well-respected scholar on Bible and oral tradition, got excited about my work, and when NBS founder Tom Boomershine said "Yes, this is a great next step for us; yes, Romans is a necessary book for us to engage with through storytelling; yes, your work is important and valuable." Richard also was right behind my project, and Phil encouraged me to share my work with the seminar. This group of scholars stayed with me throughout the PhD; I returned in 2016, though not 2017 as I was preparing to submit the thesis. In 2018, our drinks night was allowed to be appropriated by me as part of my year of turning 40 celebrations!

In the years I have been involved, I have written scholarly musings that go to the whole network, presented workshops at Festival Gatherings, and provided new translations for the seminar as we play with books and storytelling process so as to resource the network. Almost exactly as I was handing my thesis in, the committee were meeting after the Festival Gathering and planning future gatherings, and before I had even defended my thesis, let alone passed, I had been invited to be our keynote speaker in 2020. For 2023, when the epic telling was Romans, the seminar looked to me as one who has been deeply immersed in it, to lead us in much of our work of preparing it for the epic.[6]

I have enjoyed a range of collaborations with members of the network and seminar over the years. One has been to record portions of the Bible for a friend writing biblical studies for a resource produced by their denomination. I was invited to tell a story and reflect on the meaning I found there for a student from India in the Academy of Biblical Storytelling, and my work for the 2020 gathering was influential on another student of the Academy and her major project. The Masters program for the Academy includes my Embodied Performance Analysis method in the syllabus. I connected a PhD student in New York with the Network and seminar, who I first met in Edinburgh, then met with by Zoom to reflect on her doctoral work with her. I have been invited to supervise the thesis of a Masters student in Australia who is a member of the Network, and to consult with a student of another seminar member on a major liturgy project. I led worship (remotely) during the 2021 Festival Gathering, and composed the closing liturgy for our Seminar convenor when Phil ended his time in that role in 2022.

Members of the seminar helped with my PhD thesis in various ways, in addition to the conversations and encouragement I have mentioned. In 2016, Jason Chesnut filmed me telling a section of Romans 1, then edited the video as we explored a different way of telling a part of the letter that has been used to cause harm to LGBTQI+ folk in its interpretation and application.[7] Kathy Maxwell read a thesis chapter for me, to provide feedback

---

6. The "Epic Telling" is a whole book or large section of the Bible broken into smaller portions and presented by multiple tellers, in order, usually in a 1–2 hour performance. nbsint.org/pages/epic-telling

7. Sarah Agnew with Jason Chesnut, "03. Romans 1 Digital Storytelling", 2017.

from another perspective than my supervisor. Richard Swanson examined the thesis and provided a forward for the book, and Tom Boomershine provided an endorsement for the book also. The affirmation of my work through such participation is a gift in each event, and in the collective welcome and nurture of my scholarly voice as a storyteller.

In 2015, I offered a workshop on Romans 16 and embodied performance at the Festival Gathering. Participants talked so highly of it that the numbers for the second offering of the workshop exploded to standing room only! Some still talk of it, and the impact it has had on their own telling practice. I heard of one teller who was inspired to also tell Romans 16 after that workshop. This is a little bit amazing because Romans 16 is essentially a list of greetings from Paul and his companions to various folk in the church in Rome. My embodied performance interpretation led me to translate the Greek differently to the NRSV, which I mostly used in this work. Where they used "greet" I used "embrace," and the gesture that accompanied my speaking of the letter aloud here was a reaching out with my right hand, as if to cup the face of a beloved friend or relation. A list of formal greetings was transformed by this translation into messages of love and kinship; into an embodiment of the letter's exhortations to embrace and "love one another" (13:8, 9), "welcome one another" (14:1) "with mutual affection" (12:10) and "as Christ has welcomed you" (15:7), to enact the mutuality of reconciled, healing, relationship that Jesus himself lived.[8]

For a number of seminars, I have provided translations for the Biblical passages which I or other tellers have performed in our workshops—you have seen my translation of Micah 6:1–8. We play with parts of the portion chosen for the epic in the following year, so that we might equip the storytellers with insights and questions, to help their preparation. I have heard from seminar members appreciation for my translations that are poetic, and especially their use of expansive language for God (Holy One, and They/Them/ Their pronouns).

It was a particular honor to be the keynote speaker for the 2020 Festival Gathering, introducing learning from my doctoral studies in embodiment and performance. A few months after the keynotes—which of course were delivered by pre-recording on Zoom rather than trying to deliver them live late at night or very early morning, because I was stuck in Australia in the first year of the pandemic, and the Festival Gathering takes

---

sarahagnew.com.au/Embodied-Performance.

8. See Agnew, *Embodied Performance*, Chapter 6 for a fuller discussion of my Performance Analysis of Romans.

place in the USA—my thesis book was published. *Embodied Performance* has had a small but engaged audience. And as with so much of what I write, I have no idea really how far it has travelled, or what impact it is having. But I know a few people have read it, engaged with it, and watched the video that is Chapter 5 of the book. There are even a couple of reviews published.[9] And in 2025, the conversation continues as students at the Academy for Biblical Storytelling engage with a chapter of *Embodied Performance*, and I join them as a guest contributor in their summer intensive.

Pause

Take a moment to listen to a biblical story told by one of the members of my tribe. You'll find a library of videos at nbsint.org/resources

In the four years after I completed my PhD, I served full time in a congregation, which left little time for more scholarly involvement than the contributions for seminar and conversations with fellow storytellers from time to time. I managed to present at a couple of conferences: an introduction to Biblical Performance Criticism in a session on that approach at the Australian Fellowship for Biblical Studies Conference, and an application of my method for preachers at the inaugural "PreachFest" homiletics conference hosted by the Uniting Church's Mission and Education unit in NSW/ACT. But as I write this book, after resigning from that congregational placement, I have been available to take on some teaching again, along with the Masters Supervision. Back in the classroom after five years, it felt like I never left. I come from a long line of teachers, two lines in fact, as they're everywhere in my extended family on both my mum and dad's sides. I have expressed this genetic predisposition to teach as a workshop facilitator, bible study leader, and in several seasons, in a theological college classroom. It is another place in which I feel at home, leading by being

---

9. A book review, for example: Daniel Mossfield, "Embracing the Subjective", *Art/s and Theology Australia*, https://artandtheology.net/2021/02/25/embracing-the-subjective-a-review-of-sarah-agnews-embodied-performance-mutuality-embrace-and-the-letter-to-rome/ 2021. And an article that engages with the work, U-Wen Low, "Who Tells the Story? Challenging Audiences through Performer Embodiment." *Religions* 14: 1040. https://doi.org/10.3390/rel14081040 2023.

present, by telling the Story with others, and inviting them to tell it with their living.

Invitation to reflect

Is story a posture you take in your various roles in life?

What gift/s does, or might, story or storytelling offer you and your community?

What might be the cause of any reluctance you feel to adopting a posture of story/telling more often?

Is there another posture you take, which my reflections on story brings to mind for you?

Do you have questions of my story or the ideas I have explored; of yourself and your story?

How will you explore your questions with curiosity? Journal, art, meditation, talking with others?

Part Three: Be

"with" is the most important word in the Christian faith.
Samuel Wells, Incarnational Ministry

A Ministry of Presence

Being with, in body

WE DO FIND IT hard to trust in being present—in simply *being*.[1] It can feel incredibly exposed to embrace the nature of our role as pastors or the ordained which is to *be*. However, all we *do* flows intentionally from who we *are*, and our being called into ordination is a call on who we *are*.[2] Profoundly in a new season, through my current placement, and even as I live with ME/Chronic Fatigue and Depression, I have found, as Nolasco puts it, a freedom in opening "to the healing power of *being with* oneself, the other, and God."[3] I started my current placement with an intentional and explicitly stated priority of *being present* with and for the congregation. Consistently, reliably, present. And after a season of instability for them, the collective sigh and relief from the nominating committee, then the congregation, has been palpable.

Through my second congregational placement a posture emerged within me of a *ministry of presence*. Rather than focus on what I saw as my deficiencies as a pastoral carer, I learnt to see what I *was* doing, *was* being present for and with people. Working from the church, and being there on days when certain groups meet there, I was present, able to pop out of my office and have a cup of coffee, stay for a chat, hear some of the stories of the week. I was present for the one who needed to talk, able to invite them to come through to my office for a chat, when they were there for a meeting, a group gathering, to pick something up.

I may not be the most pro-active pastoral carer, but I am present enough to be there when you call, to come and meet you when you need

---

1. Purnell, *Being in Ministry*, 71. as Nolasco says "being is our doing work": *Contemplative Counselor*, 19.

2. Purnell, *Being in Ministry*, 71; also 2; 148; 156.

3. Nolasco, *Contemplative Counselor*, 10.

a coffee and a chat. For a number of folk on the edges in various ways, I have been on messenger, phone, and in cafés. For folk rejected by church because of their sexuality, I have been present, I have been the church present, God present, at their weddings. At one wedding reception, I even sat at the top table, in my clerical collar, the photographs of me with the two grooms going to an AFL pride related record. We, the Uniting Church, are with you, my presence said.

Being "with" is an enactment of our inherent mutuality. There's that theme again. When I published my first collection of poetry, *On Wisdom's Wings*,[4] I knew I had to do more than tell my own story. Through poetry, *On Wisdom's Wings* tells my story of life with Depression, and of a journey of broader self-discovery. I knew that, as I had found strength and courage to be vulnerable with my story, I needed to encourage others, hold space for others, to tell their story as an invitation into healing and wellbeing. One way I did this was to join with friends Sarah and Kylie, hosting "Beat the Blues", an evening of poetry, story, and song as a fundraiser for Beyond Blue.[5] Kylie is a singer-songwriter whose work, like mine, tells the story of experience with Depression.[6] Sarah was working in the Uniting Church Solidarity and Justice unit and specifically on a campaign of raising awareness of suicide. We invited Beyond Blue ambassador Damien to tell his story between Kylie's music, my poetry, and some interactive "stations", such as a tree Bethany painted, on which we hung leaves with our hopes or prayers. I wrote this post after the event.

> It began with an idea.
> I had realized that, as a contemplative, reflective person who is not one for the rallies and protests, but for the poems, the words, I am often not actively involved in the myriad causes one could support with one's presence. As a person with limited financial resources, I haven't the means to give to these causes in support of the active folk in our community, or not as often as I would like. One, in such circumstances, might give in to guilt or complacency, either response to one's situation not at all helpful.
> So I looked at what I have, what I can offer as a contemplative, reflective person: I have poems. What resources do I have? Gifts as a storyteller and story hearer. How will I use what I have to

---

4. Agnew, *On Wisdom's Wings*.
5. Beyond Blue is a research, support, and advocacy body for people in Australia living with depression and anxiety: beyondblue.org.au.
6. kyliebricemusic.com

more actively participate in my community in response to stories of brokenness to encourage healing?

I decided that in order to give money, I would need to stop spending it on something else—and shaved my head for Lent [as I shared in "Tell"].

And I decided that as some of the poems in my book give voice to experiences of depression and healing, I would like to share that story more widely, invite others to hear my story, in case it might be encouraging to them. I found a couple of friends who also wanted to invite this sharing of stories for mutual encouragement and healing, and we dreamed up "Beat the Blues". Over the past few months, we have collaborated together and with others to create yesterday afternoon's interactive arts space to beat the blues together. Did we ever!

Kylie Brice's lyrics and marvelous voice, supported by a band of equally talented musicians, spoke of depression's impact on friends and family, and on life's repercussions for depression's ebbs and flows.

I found the way we had structured Kylie's songs to be interspersed with my poems a gentle, honest, at times confronting but ultimately hopeful invitation into story —ours and the stories of our listeners.

Damien Tann, *beyondblue* speaker, shared his story, too—the importance of hope for his journey towards health and wellbeing; the importance of community, family, connection; and his need to use language of survival rather than suffering in order to stay positive and well. We all agreed afterwards that the direct story as told by Damien provided a balance for the songs and poems to which Kylie and I gave little or no introduction.

The Cafe at The Corner Uniting Church provided their usual excellent fare of coffee, tea, hot chocolate, milkshakes and cakes—for gathering together is always enhanced by eating together!

People were provided with paper, pencils, clay, with which to respond creatively as they entered the stories, and many took up the invitation. Booklets included space for imagination and creativity, and lyrics from some of our songs and poems.

Sarah (there were two Sarahs on the team) provided an interactive station, which invited folk to name the anger and pain we often feel in response to depression, anxiety, and suicide. And folk took up this invitation.

We invited those who gathered to write a name, names, or a word of hope, on a leaf to hang on our tree of life—with thanks to Beth. Not all of us pinned a leaf to the tree, and some pinned more

Part Three: Be

than one. It felt hopeful simply seeing the bare tree transformed to life with the green leaves added.

After the formal program, people stayed and mingled, and conversation flowed for at least half an hour more. I heard that in this space folk had been both confronted and encouraged. One was inspired to return to her own poetry writing, and another expressed gratitude for the invitation to create. Many told of the way they had been moved by the honesty and artistry they had experienced. And many expressed a desire for another space like this in the future.

We raised $130 for *beyondblue*—not much, perhaps, in the scheme of things. But more importantly, people had the chance to gather together, to give voice to the difficult stories and discover they are not alone, to imagine together healing and hope. *beyondblue* is all about hope and resilience, mutual support and encouragement. Please call or go to their website to access help and resources if you or someone you love experiences depression or anxiety. It began with an idea. It began with my story, and reached out to connect to so many more, and together, we beat the blues on a wintry Sunday afternoon in Adelaide. Thank you to all who played their part.

Rolf Nolasco has learned from "Buddhist philosophy [that] the only way out of suffering is . . . through it."[7] I know this from experience. As I have developed the courage to play and make mistakes, I have also developed courage enough to stay put in the hard places of my own, and with others, to pay attention, and to find our way *through*, with gatherings of honest naming of the shadows, such as "Beat the Blues". Healing can only happen when we see and tend to the wounds. Nolasco recalls the observation from Thich Nhat Hanh

> that if you run away from suffering, you have no chance to find out what path you should take in order to get out of suffering. So our practice is to embrace suffering and look deeply into its nature . . . find out what has created the suffering . . . cut the source of nutrition for suffering, and then healing will take place.[8]

Loneliness and isolation are food sources for the suffering that is Depression; healing can take place when we gather and share our stories together. Those stories need to be honest: the stories of the shadows need to be told and heard, to help us find our way into the light. Such storytelling

---

7. Nolasco, *Contemplative Counselor*, 41.
8. Nolasco, *Contemplative Counselor*, 41.

requires courage, which we may find together; which we may find when we draw on the Story of Life. As for Nolasco, the more I have attended to a contemplative way of being, entering the Divine heart in stillness and solitude, the more capacity I have "as a host with no agenda other than to make room for [others] to breathe and find their grounding again . . . to be anchored in the moment" together.[9] "Interior silence . . . brings about an attitude of hospitality."[10] It is as Brené Brown observes: to be present with and for others, we must be present with and for ourselves. She uses the language of belonging:

> True belonging is the spiritual practice of believing and belonging to yourself so deeply that you can share your most authentic self with the world and find sacredness in both being a part of something and standing alone in the wilderness. True belonging doesn't require you to *change* who you are; it requires you to *be* who you are.[11]

Returning to Nolasco's insights, he reflects on qualities of a ministry of presence in his discussion of the Contemplative Christian counsellor. Such qualities include accompaniment, one's interior peace, stillness, silence, and solitude, finding our identity in—within—Holy One. "The counsellor's identity . . . is formed by accepting the call to self-examination and then using this interior journey to accompany" others.[12] Through the practices of nurturing our inner life, with stillness and solitude, Nolasco encourages the counsellor to find identity with God, as loved by God, and from here, to be able to offer hospitality for another to do the same.[13]

A ministry of presence is about *being* more than it is about *doing*. Being with others in community. Being with people in the living of life. Turning up. Paying attention. Being me, well, authentic, whole, and *thus* being part of the wellbeing, authenticity, wholeness of others and the community together. Mutuality. In the process of discerning the call to my new congregation in 2023, I heard the need in this community after several years of short-term supply placements, for the sustained presence of a minister among them. To know this minister would be with them for years to

---

9. Nolasco, *Contemplative Counselor*, 59.

10. Nolasco, *Contemplative Counselor*, 59.

11. Brown, *Dare to Lead*, 107—originally written for her 2017 book, *Braving the Wilderness*.

12. Nolasco, *Contemplative Counselor*, 21.

13. Nolasco, *Contemplative Counselor*, 24–25; 48–49; 51.

come; to know she will be with them, here, now. After a difficult season in my former congregation, I told them not only do I hear your need, I also need you to be with me. We are each together delighting in the mutuality of intentional, committed, presence. I am finding it liberating, almost surprisingly, to focus on the quality of presence and attention I give the congregation and its members, rather than the time or amount of "work" I am *doing*. This is a life-giving measure of my effectiveness in my role—do the people feel I am with them? Everything else flows from that.

Being with, from afar

A ministry of presence, of turning up, can be particularly challenging when chronic illness causes retreat, withdrawal, and isolation. Paradoxically, however, a ministry of presence as a practice has encouraged me to find various ways to *be* present even when I am seemingly absent.

Through poetry and my blog, I have been present with folk I both know and will never know about, in the telling of the story of my experiences of Depression and ME/Chronic Fatigue. Colleagues have shared the blog with parishioners or found it helpful themselves, living with chronic illness and needing to feel not so alone.

In 2018 the congregation in which I served hosted a commemorative event for Kristallnacht, in collaboration with the Jewish community whose synagogue is nearby. My presence was listening to the story of Kristallnacht, which I had not known before. Fire and smashed glass from Jewish homes and shopfronts on one horrific night during that horrific war. Elena Katz-Chernin had been commissioned to write a piece of music for this anniversary, to be performed at our church. My presence was encouragement, affirmation, enabling the music staff to coordinate, with my support, on behalf of our team. My presence was to compose a prayer, the liturgy, and on the night, I was to help speak the liturgy. ME/Chronic Fatigue prevented me from attending. And yet, I was still present, through my words, spoken by another, holding the people in our remembering, our sorrow, our determined hope for peace.

Golden crystal hope[14]

Hope is the gold we melt and pour
between the crystal pieces, shattered,
smatterings and scatterings beneath our feet.
Tread carefully, hold gently the shards,
bear the wounds the healing cuts.
Offer the sacred price for peace, to mend
the broken crystal at our feet.
May the Holy bless us as we go.
Amen.

Of course, with the pandemic we have all had times we have had to be present while absent: keynote speaking for 2020 Festival Gathering through recordings; witnessing funerals of dear friends in Adelaide from Canberra, or leading funerals in Canberra with folk joining from around the world. I was video-phoned in to lead the prayer I composed for a couple at their wedding, and stayed on the phone to open my own bottle of champagne for the toast with the five allowed to attend the wedding in person. I led part of my sister's wedding by Zoom, wearing my bridesmaid's dress and appearing in none of the photos, because I was not allowed into my home state at the time of her wedding.

Sometimes, the being present while absent is sufficient. And sometimes, even making the best of an awful situation is still heart-breakingly awful. Because nothing quite replaces being present, physically present, with each other. Technology helps keep us connected when we are indeed far apart, and for that we are deeply grateful. And yet. We are embodied beings. To bring those bodies, and so our *whole* selves into the same space is to connect, to enact our mutuality, the wholeness we only find *together*.

"When people are forcibly separated from their bodies (for instance, when being unaware of their bodily state) and/or when their bodies are not used to relate to others, people's lives are significantly affected in a negative way . . . 'our body is built for relationships.'"[15] As I have noted else-

---

14. Written for the commemoration of Kristallnacht by Wesley Uniting Church and the Canberra Jewish Centre, November 2018. The commemoration featured the premier performance of "To mend broken crystal . . .", by Elena Katz-Chernin, commissioned for the occasion. Kristallnacht refers to a terrible night of burning Jewish schools, homes, synagogues, and businesses in Germany, marking a significant shift in the Nazi persecution of Jews that became World War II.

15. Bargár, *Embodied Existence*, 46, citing David H. Kelsey, *Eccentric Existence. A*

where, "the sciences are demonstrating that the body's very physiology not only experiences the world through sense and movement, but interprets, responds, understands in ways our conscious minds have not the capacity for comprehending."[16] It follows that for such embodied experience of moments and each other to be mediated through screens is to inhibit meaning-making potential—let alone potential for depth of human connection. How many of us have felt "Zoom fatigue" in recent years, from the extra effort to connect with each other through a screen; and the impact of turning off into sudden isolation?

of the instant goodbyes[17]

click the red button leave
the red button end
for all
       and fall
          and fall
into chasm
         to a sudden
crash
     into lonely
            only
to climb for the start
again, but I cannot start again,
cannot launch for the heart's
wrenching again, for more
of that emotional
           upheaval

Theological Anthropology. 2 Volumes. Louisville: Westminster John Knox, 2009: 544.

16. Agnew, *Embodied Performance*, 106.

17. First published on sarahagnew.com.au. Also in *From the Mist*, Eugene, OR: Resource, 2025, 25.

Pause

Call a friend. Write a letter. Reach out and connect with another.

Being with creation

Going out into nature brings us a similar kind of connection. Nothing quite replaces engaging our senses within nature. To be physically present in nature, the blue-green ocean, blue-brown rivers, red dust desert, green, green fields and forests and mountains—this is to connect, to enact our mutuality with all creation, the wholeness we only find together.

Wendy Farley observes that although later Christians have reduced revelation to the (literal) (written) word of scripture, early on we appreciated "two revelations: the book of Scripture and the book of nature."[18] Then, "Christians conceived of revelation as directed towards the whole human person in community with all creation . . . creation itself as an essential self-communication of the divine."[19] Julia Baird, in *Phosphorescence,* claims "a love of nature is coiled within our bones, laced in our marrow, steeped in our blood."[20] Having examined outcomes of research, Baird notes that "when we are exposed to sunlight, trees, water, or even just a view of green leaves, we become happier, healthier, and stronger."[21] Green around us gives us energy, reduces stress, and lifts depression.[22] An increase in exposure to nature in your daily environment can feel like the boost to life a $10–20, 000 salary increase gives, apparently.[23]

We are of earth. We are of each other. We are of the same breath of life that animates us. We are whole in the presence of what else lives. Mutuality. So, a ministry, a practice, of presence, of being *with.*

---

18. Wendy Farley, *Beguiled by Beauty. Cultivating a Life of Contemplation and Compassion.* Louisville, KY: Westminster John Knox, 2020, 143.

19. Farley, *Beguiled by Beauty,* 143.

20. Julia Baird, *Phosphorescence. On Awe, Wonder, and Things that Sustain You when the World Goes Dark.* Sydney: Fourth Estate, 2020, 33.

21. Baird, *Phosphorescence,* 35.

22. Baird, *Phosphorescence,* 35–36.

23. Baird, *Phosphorescence,* 37.

Part Three: Be

    I have long found a sense of wellbeing when I can sit, walk, swim under the vastness of the sky. Somehow the sky draws my inner being into deeper connection with the Sacred Other, with creation, and with my own self. Looking for a rental house some years ago, a place to easily go to sit outside under the sky, near the green, was a non-negotiable. This is where I find Holy One.

∾

Pause

Go outside. Talk to a plant. Listen to the birds. Smell the roses. Put your feet in soil or sand or water. Connect. Be present.

∾

Sacred Presence

I HAVE BEEN SLOWED at various times in my life by chronic pain and illness.

As a child, I experienced migraines from time to time. Often enough as to be noticed by classmates and jeered as if I was using the excuse to skive off school. I never was. Doctors linked the migraines to underdevelopment in optic nerves, perhaps nerves adjusting as they grew into a space on the smaller side of "normal". Whatever the cause, for several years I experienced these migraines, headaches fierce and piercing in agony behind my eyes. The pain was so bad it caused me nausea, and I always threw up with it. Every time. Then I would sleep for a couple of hours, and the pain would begin to ease. I don't recall that the migraines continued much into high school, so they must have stopped around 12 years of age.

Which was handy, because at 12 years of age, two decades of acute and chronic back pain began. In PE[1] class we were in teams for a relay race on this particular day, hurdles up (we had just learnt this skill), and a sprint back. On the last hurdle, I twisted as I landed, turning for the sprint back. I made it back to the team, but collapsed when I did. My lower back had felt like it snapped. Or that's how I remember it. But I wasn't going to stop running before the finish line—we were ahead: for the first time ever, I was winning a running race! But this began years of x-rays and physiotherapy. As it turned out, I had aggravated a previous injury with that twisted awkward hurdle landing. The squashed disc in my lower back, we assumed, became squashed four years earlier, when I had fallen from a beam at gymnastics. True to form, as it would become obvious in later years, I was so easily injured it did not take a fall off the full height beam, or even a mid-height practice one. No. There's a beginners' beam, so low it's really only as far as the thickness of the beam itself from the floor. That one. I fell off that one and damaged a disk in my spine.

The injury was aggravated again, just as it was healing from the hurdle incident, when a thoughtless boy knocked me over, rushing past at school. Mum still has not forgotten, nor forgiven. I added neck injuries with show

---

1. Physical Education, aka, sport.

rides and, after school, a car accident. But during high school, I often felt isolated by the back pain; it was invisible, unlike a broken leg or arm with plaster, not understood. I missed out on experiences because I was in pain, or afraid of further injury: I didn't go on the Year 10 ski trip because even an innocuous fall might aggravate the injury again.

At 17, in first year university, I was slowed, isolated, withdrawn again by a broken leg—visible ailment at last! But this time, I found the isolation welcome. Then, as I studied mood disorders for my psychology exams, I recognized myself in the symptoms; I realized what was causing *this* withdrawal was Depression. Stress from Year 12; the loss of friendships, or major upheavals and shifts and changes between friends as we moved on from high school; betrayal by the University for which my grandfather set up student and sports associations, when Dad, who had worked there 25 years was shafted; and years of isolating invisible back pain.

But I remember, even so, deciding *not* to ask "why me?" with any of these conditions. I remember choosing not to accept the blame for the lack of healing of the back pain when a youth leader suggested I was resisting God and if I let Him [sic] in, the pain would ease. No. I chose to accept *God's* ministry of presence. Is that not what the incarnation is: God *with* us?

For me, even more particularly, Breath-Spirit is the Presence of which I have always been aware. To which I am always turning, speaking, listening—figuratively and literally, with my heart and mind, and physically with expressive glances towards the sky, the beyond. For me, in more recent years, it is Creator to whom I feel connected when I sit beneath the vastness of the sky, before the vastness of the ocean.

Presence. Sacred Presence.

And an invitation to be, myself, present.

The assurance of Presence, of Spirit with me, and having parents who did not teach us of a God who grants wishes, and I resisted. I rejected the implied blame, the assumption I had turned away from God. I trusted, as I have been able to look back over my whole life and realize I always have, that Holy One is here, all around, with us. A year or two later, that trust in Sacred presence saved my life.

The Cave

After first year Uni, the Depression eased a little. I shared how circumstances combined to bring about my first experience of Depression: recoiling from Year 12 stress and the impact of a betrayal at work for my Dad; floundering in the turmoil of friendship changes after high school; isolated again with back pain. Studying for those first year Psychology exams, I was able to name and understand what was happening for me. Then, slowly, I was able to talk about it a little with my friends, seek connection, seek joy, again. But I had not really addressed the illness, and inevitably, another experience of Depression was just around the corner.

At the start of my third year in Uni, Mum and my youngest sister joined my Dad who had moved interstate six months earlier for a new job at a different university. My middle sister and I stayed in Adelaide for our studies, at first each boarding with church friends. That year, I could have been—I so wanted to be—falling in love with that one person I ever thought I could marry. But the despair ached within, made my body and mind ache, to the point that I could only see an end to the pain in an end to my life. I would park my rusty red car in the driveway, turn off the engine, and sit for minutes almost stunned that I was here in the driveway. There was a tree on the way home I thought I was planning to speed into and crash.

On Not Hitting a Tree[2]

After "Five Thousand Acre Paddock", Philip Hodgins

1.
There was only one
tree on the corner and I
drove straight past it.

2.
Flowers mark the tree
where the car ended
up. I think to myself
that could have been me
only I would have done it
deliberately.

One night in October, I found myself at the bottom of the Depression cave with my hand on the trap door to escape.

---

2. Agnew, *On Wisdom's Wings*, 43.

Part Three: Be

sinking[3]

I sank to my chair
I stared at the telephone
the bottle of wine
the car keys

I took up the phone
I put it down

I dialed no number

I took it up
I put it down
again and again

wanting to ask
made it no easier to call

I took up the bottle
put it to my lips

I swallowed no wine

I took it up
I put it down
again and again

wanting to forget
made it no easier to drown

I took up my keys
drove holes in the table

I went nowhere

I took them up
I put them down
again and again

3. Agnew, *On Wisdom's Wings*, 28.

> wanting to crash
> made it no easier to burn
>
> away from the car keys
> the bottle of wine
> the telephone
>
> I sank into my bed

I cried myself to sleep that night, having only moved from the kitchen table after I don't know how long I had sat there because it felt time my housemate would be returning home, and I did not want to see her. See anyone. When I woke, I somehow knew I had decided to live. And the hard work began.

In the years that followed, I came to understand that I had not taken the escape option because to do so I would have been letting go of life, letting go of the Source of Life. Not—please hear me—*not* that God would have let me go, had I committed suicide. I do not believe that. What spoke volumes to me was that *I* would not let go of Holy One. I did not. I chose to hang on. I trusted that Presence. And that gave me the strength and courage to get up and climb back into fuller life.

As I was starting to learn about Depression, and my experience with it, I came across a book called *The Zen Path Through Depression*.[4] Philip Martin taught me to pay attention in the dark. To be present with myself, alone in the depths.[5]

And I did; I was. As I climbed out of the darkest cave, I paid attention. I looked down to see where I had been. I looked around at the path, the crags, the footholds on my way out. I looked up towards the light, and when I emerged, I looked closely at those who had remained on the edge of my dark, holding the light. In that is the origin of *Blue, Koala?*, the story in verse dedicated to the friends who noticed I was gone, and waited for my return.[6] In almost 30 years of living with Depression, I have continued to

---

4. Phillip Martin, *The Zen Path Through Depression*, United Kingdom: HarperCollins, 1999.

5. As we also heard from Thich Nhat Hanh earlier, the only path out of the darkness is through it, present with it, not running away or ignoring it. Ken Evers-Hood makes similar observations: *The Irrational David: The Power of Poetic Leadership*. Eugene, OR: Wipf and Stock Publishers, 2019, 210.

6. Sarah Agnew, *Blue, Koala?*. Illustrated by Grace Mitchell. (MediaCom, 2018); also available as an audiobook (Bandcamp).

pay attention. With the help of counsellors, doctors, supervisors. Through poetry—writing my own, and reading others'. With study: my English Honors thesis not only explored my own experience of Depression and that of others in poetry, but drew on psychology to explore the illness in depth.

I pay attention, learning to live well with Depression. Always learning. I have been in the 50% who after one experience of Depression have another; the 70% of those who have two experiences going on to have three; the 90% of those after experiencing Depression three distinct times who then live more with than without it for the rest of their lives, as I read in the Psychology "bible", "DSM IV", at the time.[7] The second time I started taking anti-depressants, I have stayed on them, at varying doses, for over 15 years, seeing counsellors and psychologists for various periods during that time. Whenever I am almost ready to let go of the security blanket, life gets tough enough to decide that extra layer of support is still necessary. It's OK. But one day, I would like to be free of them, and their side effects.

∽

Pause

What connects you to life? Music? A walk? Friends?

Go and do that for a bit.

∽

Healing presence

I mentioned earlier that once I had published that first poetry collection, in which the thesis poems were included, along with 10 more years of poems exploring experiences of Depression, broken hearts, healing, story, life, I knew I had to help others tell their story—of Depression in particular.

It happens gently. Subtly. When I have opportunity to name my experience, I claim it without apology or shame. It is. And when I have opportunity to speak of the months during which I was suicidal, I do; although less often, and only when I feel strong and safe. I have seen movies and plays in which a suicide is shown and I had not known it would be there. Of

---

7. *Diagnostic and Statistical Manual of Mental Disorders: DSM-IV.* Washington, D.C.: American Psychiatric Association, 1994.

course, as the story unfolded, I saw it coming—I always do, as somehow it still seems to me a legitimate option for a character to consider, when most would recoil from it and want the character to resist. But in those theatres on those occasions I was still shocked. After a particular play (*Vere (Faith)* by John Doyle) I remember sitting quite still as the lights went up and the seats around us started to empty. He jumped, on stage, "out" a window. Clever staging to make us feel as though we "watched" him jump. Dad expressed confusion from the middle seat: why wasn't I getting up? Mum knew. I hadn't said anything, but she had seen the play, and she could see me now. She reminded him that suicide was a difficult story for me to see. Another time, in a movie theatre, I'd seen a film with new friends in a new city. He hung himself. Apparently, this was a remake of an older version of the story, so if you knew that story, you knew this was in it. I did not. I felt physically ill. Over coffee with these new friends, we were talking about the film, of course. I mentioned something of my stunned response. But I had not expected to need to tell my story, or that part of it, that night. To have to trust that fragile part of me to strangers without preparation caught me off guard. It unsettled me for days after.

Why do I tell you all this now, as I tell of my practice of presence? Such presence is a practice that is a commitment. A commitment made with the publishing of the poems that tell my story of living with Depression. A commitment to my own story. And a commitment to be a hearer of stories, of the hard stories, the vulnerable stories, the stories we live in the dark. I am committed to letting people know I am not afraid of the dark. I will hold light for you, as others have done, and do, for me. I will hold your story safe: I will hold *you* safe as you tell your story. For it is in the sharing of our stories that we find healing. In the turning up, listening, bearing witness, being present that a person is nurtured, affirmed, brought towards their wholeness—and thus, all of us, together.

The world in which I live prefers the denial of suffering. But, committed to the Story of God in which I find hope and healing, I know myself called—commanded, invited—to offer a healing presence to others. And I find in that commitment the desire to deepen my connection with Sacred Love, so I can be anchored there as I am present with the folk I am called to care for, and offer love. I know how to play, to imagine; thus I cultivate empathy. I understand story; thus I hold space for the stories of others. I know myself: a person adept at self-reflection, nurturing inner peace, I am always nurturing my capacity to be present—to *be*.[8]

As Purnell observes, the pastor's role is to *be,* to be with. For Nolasco, it is accompaniment. "Everything suffers. Whatever capacity a creature has for feeling its environment will cause it pain as well as pleasure," observes Wendy Farley.[9] I understand now my role as a human and as a storyteller, a poet, a minister, to be accompaniment; I see in myself the gifts and experience that enable me to hold space for another to feel safe in telling the story of their being in its flaws and "failures", as much as its joys and delights.[10] So let me tell you something more of my story in its struggle and how I met the next set of challenges.

Pause

Who accompanies you?

To whom to you offer accompaniment?

What is the gift in that, for you?

---

8. We will hear echoes in here from my conversation partners, Doug Purnell (*Being in Ministry*, 13, 63); Rolf Nolasco (*Contemplative Counselor*, 29, 112); Brian Edgar (*God Who Plays*, 12).

9. Farley, *Beguiled by Beauty*, 124.

10. Julia Baird reminds us of the importance of this, as does Brené Brown: Baird, *Phosphorescence*, 86; Brown, *Dare to Lead*, 179.

Chronically Fatigued

> Part of validating your own story is finding your voice and claiming your authority, especially for the women and introverts among us. And a crucial part of all this is the need to accept your imperfections, to shrug off lame dictates about how to dress and the need to please, and to stop beating yourself up when you don't feel #blessed or #well and you are really feeling more like #FML or #everythingiscrap.[1]

IT WAS IN SCOTLAND that I started to wonder if I might be experiencing what I knew as Chronic Fatigue Syndrome (CFS). I was tired. So. Very. Tired. No energy to do things. Feeling a lack of capacity to do things. I pulled out of social engagements a lot. People wore me out. I found walking too far—more than ten minutes sometimes—not only made me tired, it made my entire body ache for days. As if my muscles were inflamed. As if my bones were inflamed. It diminished my capacity to think clearly. I didn't absorb anything I read. I found it terribly difficult to create, to write, to imagine, to learn stories for performing. And I was in Scotland to do a PhD—lots of reading and writing. A PhD on performing the Bible—so I had a book of the Bible to learn and perform.

I had been living with experiences of Depression for twenty years by now. The Depression was also worsening—I was almost catatonic on my bed a number of times, incapacitated by fatigue, pain, grief, dread—*and* what I was experiencing was new, was different, was more than what it had been before.

I have since learned to name this as *Myalgic Encephalomyelitis* (ME, or ME/CFS). The myalgia is chronic muscle pain; the encephalomyelitis is swelling in the brain and spinal cord. Much more serious than the excessive tiredness suggested when we call it "Chronic Fatigue". In fact, that chronic fatigue is the major symptom, as ME causes a dysregulation in the body's energy production at a cellular level. Those with ME (and Long Covid,

---

1. Baird, *Phosphorescence*, 86–87.

which is very similar) have less energy, use it up quickly, and replenish it slowly. The other symptoms of ME include cognitive impairment, cold and flu symptoms, glandular pain and/or swelling, body temperature dysregulation, difficulty being upright for too long; and Long Covid has some slightly different symptoms that flow from the particularities of Covid-19. A major part of the illness is what is called Post-Exertional Malaise (malaise is another understatement); I call it a "crash". This is when all those symptoms intensify after we do something. By do something, I mean walk, cook, laugh, cry, concentrate . . . it differs each and every time, and for every person, and is impossible to predict. When it happens, all I can do is stop, rest for a day, a week, a month; and then re-set the management strategies I have developed over the decade with which I know I have lived with it. Beginning in Scotland during the PhD.

The circumstances in which the Fatigue was worsening were: single person in a foreign country alone; doing a big thing every PhD student doubts, often, they can do at all; with short-term funding and the constant pressure to find more if the project was to continue. And that person came to Edinburgh already living (albeit well) with Depression.

The stress was debilitating.

Doctors worked through the steps with me towards diagnosing ME/CFS, which is a process of elimination of all the testable conditions it *could* be with those symptoms. There is no test for ME itself. Research has been slow to develop, as the condition is so complex and unpredictable. One positive to emerge from our devastating experiences with Covid-19 is an increase in resources and attention towards Long Covid, and by extension the related ME/CFS.

The symptoms eased some, when the financial stress eased with enough to get me to the end of a third year, to submission and examination and *viva*. For the ones who made that possible, I am forever and deeply grateful.

When I returned to Australia, it was to another bundle of stressors. I moved country, then cities—Edinburgh to Adelaide to Canberra. I experienced grief at leaving Edinburgh and the friends I'd made over those three years. And the usual low that one experiences when a big, intense period of life comes to an end (many PhD graduates know this to be true). There was a new grief at leaving Adelaide again. When I left the first time, it was for three years, with uncertainty about what would come next. Now, it was for seven to ten years, or more. Would I ever live in Adelaide again?

Friendships had changed in my absence, and there would be more grief as many would be let go, or become long-distance in more than geography, but time, presence, energy. Then there is the stress, joy-filled though it was, of starting a new job and settling into a new place. By the time I found a new GP with whom to describe the Depression and Chronic Fatigue (as I was still calling it), I had also come down with Glandular Fever, which was followed by post-viral fatigue.

In a new place, being isolated and incapacitated by chronic illness is far from ideal. I couldn't explore the city, or make new friends, for the pain and the lack of energy.

What I *could* do, however, was learn to live as well as possible with these two chronic illnesses. I had been doing that for 25 years with Depression, an old dog sleeping in the corner these days, stirring only occasionally. Now, with more resources available, I explored what practices would help me find healing with the Fatigue.

Rest

Listening to a friend who has lived with this longer than I, I knew that when the pain and fatigue are at their worst, doing nothing is the thing you must do. Move your body and your mind as little as possible. That is the only way they will heal so you may move again, think again with any strength, freedom, or sustainability. I have developed quite a capacity to sit and do nothing for long periods of time.

As pain began to ease, I added in listening to audio books. I sat at a table and did jigsaw puzzles, or lay on the couch, listening to novels and autobiographies and poetry.

In pursuit of minimizing how much my body had to move, I had groceries delivered, pre-prepared dinners delivered, and I employed someone else to clean my house.

I no longer went for walks. Walking had been in former times a gentle exercise my fragile body could cope with, and a practice I appreciated and enjoyed. The sermons and poems I composed, or at least began, when walking through my neighborhood, by creeks, around a volcano, or by the beach. The being in creation, the deepening of breath in fresh air, the vitamins from the sun. Walking nurtures my body, frees my mind, connects me with the Divine. The challenge of ME/CFS is that moving hurts, if not in the moment, then two days after. This is the Post-Exertional Malaise (PEM) I mentioned. The paradox is that gently moving can help to build strength and encourage healing.

I began to feel a strong pull towards water: warm water. Hot baths had helped when I lived with chronic back pain through my teens and twenties, and been soothing through Depression's deep valleys. The bath at the manse was not, I confess, appealing. More, though, I suspected being in deeper water might help me to move, be held, warmed, soothed. Those resources I now had included access to loans through the church's financial structure. I took out a loan and purchased a spa-pool, receiving permission from the congregation to install it in the double garage at the manse. Not the prettiest of settings, it was nevertheless an established concrete slab on which to safely place the six thousand liter, car-sized pool, and enclosed enough to keep warm through the icy Canberra winters, and the hunch I had was indeed accurate. In the water, I began to move. At first, it was simply sweeping arms and legs through the bubbling water as I sat in the spa seats. Gradually, I began to swim. Short laps (it was 4 meters in length, with 4 spa seats at one end) of breast stroke. Over the months, on a tether, I added five minutes, then ten, of solid, ever stronger, back stroke. It helped. More than anything else I did during those years, this helped. The spa was both rest and movement; in stillness and solitude, I began to experience some rehabilitation. After three years, I began to be able to go for short walks again, too, with water to soothe and strengthen on the days between. Rest is not only absence of movement; it is also a gentle, slow quality to our moving into healing.

Rhythm

"The contemplative life is richly fed by deliberate practices of meditation and prayer."[2] By patterns of thinking, by intentional postures, or habits, of paying attention, being present. It is all training ourselves to be open to the Sacred and the world; aligning ourselves to the Story we choose to follow, embody, enact.[3] I don't do so well with the carving out of set times for practices, but I did take the opportunity of this illness to develop a more mindful, attentive, contemplative way of being. I started with rhythm, a rhythm for my weeks that might support sustained energy.

---

2. Farley, *Beguiled by Beauty*, 139.
3. Farley, *Beguiled by Beauty*, 139

I had a long practice of shaping my days in three sections: morning, afternoon, evening. Seven days; three sections each. For one day a week, I would rest for all three sections. For four days a week I would work two out of three sections, and rest for one. For two days a week, work one, rest two (although Sunday 'rest' is actually the recovery part of the work of the morning). And in that order. The table below shows you what it looks like for a typical week when I work full time. This is from 2023, with the two roles in congregation and theological college.

	AM	PM	E
Mon	REST	REST	REST
Tues	WORSHIP PREP and ADMIN	REST	CHURCH MEETING
Wed	WORSHIP PLANNING	WORSHIP PLANNING	FAMILY DINNER
Thurs	CLASS PREP	TEACHING	REST
Fri	MARKING / ADMIN / CLASS PREP	PASTORAL VISIT	REST
Sat	SERMON PREP	LUNCH WITH FRIENDS OR ADMIN	REST
Sun	GATHERED WORSHIP	RECOVERY	REST

In other seasons ME/Chronic Fatigue has needed a different rhythm:

One day: work none, rest three.
Two days: work two, rest one.
One day: work one, rest two.
One day: work two, rest one.
Two days: work one, rest two.

PART THREE: BE

	AM	PM	E
Mon	REST	REST	REST
Tues	STAFF MEETINGS and ADMIN	REST	CHURCH MEETING
Wed	WORSHIP PLANNING	WORSHIP PLANNING	REST
Thurs	PASTORAL CONVERSATIONS	REST	REST
Fri	SERMON PREP / ADMIN	PASTORAL VISIT	REST
Sat	SERMON PREP / PASTORAL	REST	FAMILY DINNER
Sun	GATHERED WORSHIP	RECOVERY	REST

Still only one full day off a week. But in that placement, I would often work two sections on a work-one-section day. Something had to change, so for six months, I had two extra days with an extra section for rest. And that did amount to another day off per week, as I reduced my workload and pay to 0.8 full time equivalent. Once I returned to full time, I set those two afternoons aside for the work of reading or other light tasks, intentionally taking a slower pace to manage my energy levels. With that rhythm, I found I did not need to take longer periods of rest—or sick leave—for one, two, or three weeks at a time, as I had in the years before this. So long as stress levels did not heighten. Can you hear Morgan Freeman's narration: "Inevitably, Sarah would experience heightened levels of stress"?

In 2024, I again had to adjust. I could not sustain two part-time roles; could not cope with a full-time load. Especially when I was living that expectation in the church that "full time" for ministry agents means six days per week. It seems I have only capacity for part-time, and am now only working the 0.7 FTE placement with the congregation. This gives me two full days for rest, along with the half days, and as I am required on duty for two or three Sundays each month, I also have some full weekends for rest, which this congregation understand to be to some extent part of my being present with them (and recovering time in lieu for the spilling over of life into rest time, as is inevitable in such a role as mine). Not that I am counting the hours I "work": remember I have observed a shift in this current placement, measuring my effectiveness with the quality of my presence. These weekly planning sheets still help me manage my time, or more, my energy. When am I present with the congregation, and when am I taking the necessary time to withdraw, rest, and replenish? It is a constant striving for balance.

Balance

I have found practices with food to be helpful, with ME/Chronic Fatigue. Minimizing dairy, gluten or high GI foods, sugar, caffeine, and alcohol. All the fun things, I know. The tricks are to minimize, not eliminate, and to make one change at a time. To find balance. For a number of years, I have held to these practices, and when I do, I sustain wellbeing, and minimize the physical pain of ME/CFS.

One more thing, which is also connected to rhythm, is the balance of time I spend with people and in solitude. When I went through formation for ordination, I participated in a leader's retreat. One activity we were guided through was the Myers-Briggs personality scale. I have studied psychology, so I know that possibly what such tests test best is one's ability to do a test, and to do *that* test in particular. However, I found, and continue to find, it helpful to reflect on what that test showed me of who I am and how I participate in the world. My result: I/E NFP. Yes, I know you usually have either an I *or* an E. But I am not fudging my results when I tell you I was exactly even on the Introvert / Extrovert scale.

Before I go further with the I and the E, the other letters refer to iNtuition, Feeling and Perception. I understand that I find my way by emotion or affect or instinct; feeling my way through processes, essays, creativity, tasks, life. I see it as a strength, and I play to that strength.

Applying it to study or other writing tasks, I understand that what I am doing when I seem to be procrastinating is allowing my subconscious to feel my way into understanding, into the shape of the argument, the piece of work at hand. Whereas once I felt guilty and resisted it, now I work with it. I prepare early with research and drafts and give myself time for procrastination. I use cross stitch, coloring, the dishes, a swim or walk or nap, to distract my consciousness and liberate the intuition, feeling, and perception to do the work they do best. I later leaned into such embodied knowing for my doctoral work, my examination of embodied performance *as* interpretation of the Bible, intuition *as* a tool for meaning making, as I have mentioned earlier.

Back to the I/E split: it surprised me at first. I can't remember, but I think I was expecting to find myself to be more Introvert, as I spend so much time in my own world. But that's the feeling, perhaps. I was exactly even on Introvert and Extrovert, and over the years since, I have found it helpful to consider myself an "ambivert": one who needs a balance of solitude and company for well-maintained energy. Most of us do, I suppose: I am one for whom it's generally needed to be quite even. For one's intro/extra-vertedness is less about how shy or gregarious one is, and more about whether you are energized by being alone or with other people. And for me, it has been, on reflection, a fairly even balance of solitude and company. Until ME/Chronic Fatigue, that is. While the Depression seemed to be affected by any imbalance of equal (wakeful) time with people and without, the ME/CFS has actually changed what a healthy balance looks like for me. Time with others is less energizing than it used to be, more likely to drain energy sooner than it once did. These days, I am more introverted than extroverted—though I am still aware of the need to connect beyond myself, with other humans, with creation, and of course, with the Divine. Solitude has become, then, another vital practice in my living well with ME/Chronic Fatigue. And the people time is as vital as ever for living well with Depression. It is indeed a constant striving for balance.

Lament

Remember the narrator's "Sarah would experience heightened stress" from above? Stress upsets the balance, as I am sure you have unfortunately discovered, and usually just as you have found it. When a particularly stressful situation that sustained over two years got to the point of unmanageable, even unjust, I ended up not only with ME/Chronic Fatigue worsening, but Depression also worsening, and then Burn Out. And the burn further compounded everything else. Eventually this situation came to a head, and it was no longer healthy for me to remain in that placement. When I resigned, and came home to Adelaide to stay at mum's, I completely fell into brokenness.

I had not created for four or five months by then.
I could not think.
I was in pain, and fatigued: utterly, utterly exhausted of all energy.

I was incapacitated, and the gift I gave myself, and received from mum and my close family and friends, was permission to *be* as I was. To *be* depleted and not need to pretend otherwise. To tell the story, with care for other parties, and for not repeating trauma for myself, and be heard. To take time to lie broken before I was ready to pick up pieces and heal. And when I was ready, to take small steps, and stop, withdraw, start again, as I needed.

Thinking about it now, this might have been an embodied lament. A seeing things as they truly are.[4] A naming of pain, anger, disappointment, betrayal, and bringing it to God. A sitting in the discomfort, and having company there. A walking through the valley, the tunnel, the dark, as the way back into light, into life.

Being.

Being broken without shame.

Being lost without fear.

Being me when who I am had been so recently under fire.

Reading Ken Evers-Hood[5] on lament, I am struck by the way we need courage—and we need presence—in order to practice lament. We need courage, for lament is painful, and it is counter-cultural. As Evers-Hood notes, America (and I would add, Australia), doesn't want lament: "grieving might bring about something worse."[6] This needs presence, too: Evers-Hood is exploring the story of King David in the Hebrew Bible / Old Testament: "David knows how to lament because David knows how to see and listen to the world around him."[7] My being present to, and with, my brokenness, was yet courageous. I am grateful for all I have been, grown to become, that enabled courage to guide my response in that particular season.

And perhaps I was for myself the contemplative counsellor Rolf Nolasco describes, embodying "a non-anxious presence, unconditional acceptance, and an unflinching belief in the power of faithful accompaniment in bringing about healing and transformation."[8] For I was intentionally, deliberately, present to my grief and pain in these months. Not to wallow, but rather to listen, so the grief and the pain were heard. Eventually, I asked a spiritual director to hold space with me, so that I could place the anger

---

4. Evers-Hood, *Irrational David*, 209.
5. Evers-Hood, *Irrational David*, 207.
6. Evers-Hood, *Irrational David*, 207.
7. Evers-Hood, *Irrational David*, 209.
8. Nolasco, *Contemplative Counselor*, 67.

and grief between us, attend to them, see what else they held, in order to finish the story and put it back on the shelf. Part of me, but not clamoring for attention in ways that would inhibit my wellbeing or my offering of hospitable presence to others.

Douglas Purnell describes a process of letting go of his grief, when he preached a particular sermon with a prayer to be forgiven and forgiving people; he describes becoming "somehow set free," afterwards throwing out papers connected to a job he had lost in a sudden and hurtful way some time before.[9] In the process of presence and attentiveness to the people now before him, those for whom his pastoral and preaching presence was nourishing their souls, this minister found inner peace, healing, and a way to let go. His story resonated with my own as I reflected on my grieving and letting go.

In his theological reflections on our embodied existence, Pavol Bargár also describes the courage of lament. To steadfastly see, acknowledge, and remain with pain and suffering, to name the suffering and sorrow, opens a path, he suggests, to healing.[10] Further, when we lament *together*, we "stand in solidarity with those who suffer and offer hope to the desperate" as acts of hope, bearing witness to God's hopeful presence with us.[11]

~

None of this is a template for anyone else's wellbeing, except for the practice of listening, of paying attention to *how* and *who* you are and putting into practice habits and rhythms to sustain *your* wellbeing and becoming. All of this was, finally, after years of an inkling of, but not enough commitment to, a desire to live according to a contemplative way.

---

9. Purnell, *Being in Ministry*, 125.
10. Bargár, *Embodied Existence*, 147.
11. Bargár, *Embodied Existence*, 147.

Pause

What are you hearing?

How are you feeling?

Where is my story meeting you in yours?

A contemplative way of being

Do you remember the calling into solitude I mentioned? My choice not to seek a spouse led my mum to comment one day: "If the Uniting Church had convents, I could see you becoming a nun." Which may seem strange alongside her sorrow when I informed her she would not get to satisfy her curiosity about how I would be a mother. But she is not wrong. A convent *would* be one way to be solitary in community. A suitable order. A suitable rule.

But there's where I run into an obstacle. I have told you of finding rhythm, of rhythm being necessary. But the shape of my days needs flexibility, fluidity, for me to go with the feelings. I suspect a rule of daily offices strictly kept to time would not be so life-giving for me, long term. I quite like the structure of residential conferences and retreats, in the short term. But eventually, I would feel constricted.

It is not only the singleness or solitude within community that appeals to me, about the life of a nun, however. There's the closeness, attentiveness, to the Sacred; the practices of stillness, quiet, contemplation and prayer of various orders that seems attractive to me. Contemplative. And yes, quiet. I can spend a whole day in silence: not speaking, not turning on radio or television or music. I actually dislike noise, too much of it, or at certain times of the day. Mornings especially. It is another reason living alone works best for me: I can control what noise in the house, and when (though not, of course, the noise from outside that disrupts from time to time, such as the flock of peafowl—yes peacocks and hens—who were my neighbors for four years, but that's another story).[1]

A practice I have taken on at various times is to sit outside—sometimes with coffee or wine, sometimes with nothing at all—and look up and out to the sky, the trees, and breathe. I did it occasionally without understanding why it felt important, as a teenager, on the patio at the house I grew up

---

1. In the Peacock's Roost podcast, I explored learning to live well with unwelcome circumstances—such as peacocks on the roof, and Chronic Fatigue: Sarah Agnew, "Peacock's Roost": soundcloud.com/sarahtellsstories/sets/peacocks-roost-season-1

in. I even changed rooms, from a big one to the small one decorated for my much younger sister, for her view out to those hills. Later, in a house I shared with a friend, I would sit on the patio and watch storms over the ocean and Kaurna plains; in Edinburgh I sat in the deep window sill looking out to a sun- or rain-drenched Arthur's Seat and the Salisbury Crags or, in winter, through bare trees and falling snow to the Firth of Forth. In Canberra, I put a chair on the small front porch, and sat there on winter afternoons in the sun, or for breakfast before the day warmed up in summer. It needs to be somewhere I can see the sky, and if I can see water, too, all the better. But sky. I seem to need to reach into the sky as I contemplate, seek presence, with the Sacred. I suppose it's why I like walking, as much as sitting. To reach into the air, the Breath, the Spirit. I told you earlier that have always known the Sacred near me as Spirit, as Breath, especially.[2]

The more I practice the stepping outside, the taking of the moment to be still, the presence in creation, the more it changes my posture overall. I am more present, pay more attention, carry stillness—or peace—within. Is that what it is to live a contemplative way? It's not a strict structure, they're not set times every day. It is a rhythm, in its way, a fluid structure; chords on which to play.

The jazz keeps playing

If you will indulge me, I would like to lean into the striving for balance, rhythm, intuition, and flexibility, I've mentioned; into chords and improvisation. I would like to tell you more about a metaphor I've carried with me for so much of life: jazz. I wrote this from the Greenbelt Festival in 2008:[3]

> Was Jesus a jazz musician? This was the title of the first session I attended on my last day of the festival. The speaker, Philip Roderick, is involved with a group called contemplative fire, who had led some worship sessions that I had missed, and it was too late by now to do anything about that. However, coordinating a jazz church space as I do (Black Wood Jazz), I thought I would hear someone else's reflections on Jesus and jazz.

---

2. I love that in both the Hebrew and Greek of the Bible, the same word is used for Breath and Spirit: *ruach* in Hebrew, *pneuma* in Greek.

3. On sarahtellsstories.blogspot.com 25 August 2008. Greenbelt is a Christian arts and social justice festival held at the time on the Cheltenham racecourse. greenbelt.org.uk

Part Three: Be

Really there was nothing new in what Philip said, using language for Jesus and jazz such as flow, zone, grace, and swing. There is a dance between structure and freedom in jazz, as there was in the life of Jesus, in what he was teaching the disciples. As he, as we, allow the Spirit to speak/flow through structures, the both/and-ness of things is beautiful.

All of creation has a melody—we need to listen, to hear. As we interact with others, Philip suggests that it is helpful to find their melody and thus be able to walk in time with them.[4]

Improvisation is hugely underestimated, Philip said, before going on to speak about *bricolage*. This is a French word for taking what we have and using just that, and then he led us in an improvisation singing *vive la bricolage*. It was lovely. We sang the phrase or the word in our own melodies and harmonies, listening and responding to each other in a moment of magic. As community we strive to breathe together, think together, pray together in improvisation. Again, the image of community mirrors that of a jazz band, with its delicate balance of personalities, each individual and each group learning the best of the past and adding our own personal vision. One has to understand one's own role in the group well enough in order to improvise.

Philip spoke of three elements of a jazz musician: respect for tradition (learning not merely repeating); respect for other players, allowing each person's gifts to blossom; openness to learning something new from an old piece and from each other. Are these elements in all people, living in community?

Relating jazz to the kingdom, Philip suggests that in neither is there failure—only feedback. Jazz operates on the knife-edge of failure, *incorporating* mistakes and bum notes.

And on contemplative prayer, he says that this requires the same attentiveness, attunement and alertness that jazz calls for in order for music to play the performer, in order for us to be *played through*.

Philip played a hang drum (more commonly known now as the handpan) at various intervals during the session—it's a wonderful sound.[5] "The hang drum is one of the very few newly designed musical instruments. With its ancestry in the Caribbean steel drum, this extraordinarily evocative percussion instrument

---

4. In later years I would remember this idea, as I learned more about story, and the respect for another as the expert of their story.

5. Sam Maher is a gifted Australian hand pan musician—look him up at sam-maher.com.

looks like a wok with a view or a small UFO! Its tonal quality is healing and ambient."[6]

Some time later, watching a video in the "Nouma" series,[7] I called this talk to mind, this thinking about the body of Christ as a jazz band. In it, Rob Bell makes a similar point about how we each listen to the Song and to each other, striving for harmony and balance, offering both ourselves and the invitation to others to be themselves.

> Rob Bell sits up on the balcony in a theatre while a small orchestra plays a really simple song. The music begins with a keyboard; guitar and piano join in, then strings, wind, and eventually drums and bass. It is magic. The music builds as Bell wonders about where God is, how we understand God, how we have in Jesus a tangible image of God to help us to find our way back into relationship with God. Jesus' way of love, compassion, justice, healing—"I can relate to that, I can understand that—I can sing that tune." The music builds again as the strings enter the song, and Bell pauses—and a tear rolls down my cheek.
>
> The camera pans around the theatre, taking in different views of the orchestra, and I am struck once again by a collection of musicians playing together as a picture of the body of Christ. This is what God calls humanity towards—this is what the realm of God is—an orchestra playing God's Song, the Song going on, inviting each of us to join it, to offer ourselves to the Song as we also make space for others to enter the Song, valuing each "instrument" for its unique sound . . . listening as much as we are singing/playing.[8]

And then, as I set a rhythm for a new year in Scotland, I wrote:

> A new year and new semester means establishing a new chord structure and a new rhythm for my weeks.
>
> This semester, Tuesdays are going to be "sarah tells stories" days—one day a week set aside amidst the primary work of the PhD to ensure that other projects—a new poetry collection and the storytelling show (in)humanity—continue to progress.
>
> Weekends will be time off, with a bit of story and poetry thrown in, no doubt, and study when deadlines loom.
>
> I am quite intuitive, feeling, perceiving, which means I like to go with how I am feeling in the moment—do I feel like studying,

---

6. contemplativefire.org/store.html

7. Rob Bell, "Nooma 011: Rhythm – Rob Bell". Produced by Zondervan. YouTube, Aug. 20 2012. https://youtube/1FNHoYl8a78?si=iAtKTrFCxLom_E-D

8. First published on sarahtellsstories.blogspot.com 8 August 2010.

I will study, do I feel like walking, I will walk . . . but I have found that setting a structure around which to work allows the work to actually get done. It's a bit like the chord structures around which a jazz musician improvises, and as a person engaged in multiple pursuits in any one season of life, this image has become a very useful tool. Parameters guard against chaos, encourage harmony and beauty.

So, on a study day I set the chords for my intuitive feeling my way by asking where is the energy for the various tasks within the study schedule—reading, writing, conference or journal papers, etc.? On a story/poetry day, I will spend time on whichever project the creative juices are stirring over. Was it Jung who recognized that for any strength, there is a shadow side? If I only went with what I feel like doing, some necessary tasks might be neglected. Giving myself a structure, I recognize my strength in intuition and perception, that I work by feeling my way, and enhance it by providing the chords through each movement that *needs* to be played.[9]

I found jazz in high school, exploring its origins for my final year music independent study. This study drew on my family's welcome of PhD students from far-off places, as I explored African roots to jazz by interviewing a drummer we had come to know through a PhD student, both from The Sudan. I invited Sam to give a workshop on drumming from his tradition with my classmates. The study further connected me with my Dad, and showed me a shared intensity in our music appreciation. I listened again and again to his CD of Paul Simon's collaborations with the South African musicians Ladysmith Black Mambazo (*Graceland*). This deep dive into jazz and its roots taught me not only of chords and improvisation, but of resistance, of struggle, as I learnt of the birth of jazz and blues in the gospel singing of the enslaved in America.

I started this reflection on jazz with the question of Jesus as a jazz musician. Resisting. Singing a counter-cultural song of hope through troubles. Rising from death into life. Oh, yes, Jesus and jazz go hand in hand; Jesus and jazz both teach me how to sing the Sacred song.

---

9. First published on sarahtellsstories.blogspot.com 13 January 2015.

Pause

Take time to be silent. A moment, and hour, a day. What do you notice?

Listen to some more jazz. Or handpan. Or a song you can sing to, with feeling.

A Rule of Sacred Presence

> Silence is not obscene, it is presence.
>
> Julia Baird, *Phosphorescence*

For Wendy Farley, contemplation "is a way to inhabit ordinary life. . . . A contemplative way of life reorients our awareness to the [Divine] presence that is always with us."[10] And we can do this more in the everyday the more we practice in moments apart for stillness, silence, and solitude. It is taking a posture, being intentional in paying attention. In our increasingly noisy world, Julia Baird reminds us that

> we need to reach for those tiny drops of stillness. . . . I often find them when I dive into water, when I walk the dog, when I stop to sit on a bench and look at the sky, when I sink into my mat at the end of a yoga class, when I curl up with a cup of tea on my porch.[11]

Some speak of mindfulness—for Brené Brown it is paying attention, and Nolasco talks of inclining the ears of our heart towards God.[12] The point is to look, to cultivate an openness so as to find it, "alone, but not afraid" in your recovery bed after surgery.[13]

As you can see, for many years now, I have been playing with a way of being that tells a story of hope and life. That call to solitude, a kind of

---

10. Farley, *Beguiled by Beauty*, xiii, xiv.
11. Baird, *Phosphorescence*, 75.
12. Brown, *Dare to Lead*, 149; Nolasco, *Contemplative Counselor*, 22.
13. Baird, *Phosphorescence*, 258.

Part Three: Be

monasticism, lived out through a rule that works for me. A rule of life is just like jazz chords, providing structure to hold the improvising of life in balance. Our identity "is closely tied to the pursuit and regular practice of spiritual disciplines,"[14] so what do my spiritual disciplines look like, as an intuitive, feeling, person? How are the rhythms of my days nurturing alignment with the Holy?

Some years ago now, I considered what are the postures or practices or attitudes that I want to feature in each day of my living, and I shaped those postures into my own "rule". There are seven practices to which I commit, disciplines that I find align me with the Way of the Divine. I am calling them my Rule of Sacred Presence:

> stillness
> movement
> listening
> using my voice
> being in creation
> loving
> receiving love.

At the close of each day, I take a moment (and if I have not been still before now, here is the practice of stillness for the day), and write briefly how I have been still, moved, listened, used my voice, been in creation (or nature), loved and been loved.

You may notice that I do not list a specific daily practice that names God or the Bible. The underpinning for this rule *is* a seeking of Holy One, and the shaping of the Sacred Story. This rule presents these practices as ways of enacting God's Sacred Story. I later amended my "Gifts of the Week" reflection on the week as a whole to use the postures that shape this book's telling of my story. On Sundays, I add these extra prompts for reflection on the week:

> Play
> Tell
> Be
> Holy One

Where and how have I been at play? Innovative, creative, failing, flying, finding delight and choosing joy? Where and how have I encountered and engaged in story? Where and how have I been present—with others, with the Sacred, for myself? Beneath and through it all, how have I connected,

14. Nolasco, *Contemplative Counselor*, 22.

attended to, the Holy? For I did find, as I more regularly engaged with this practice, that I wanted to specifically name Holy One's presence in my living.

You may also notice in this rule the pause before acting for myself. I am still before I move; I listen before I speak; I love before—or more properly here, *as* I am also loved. The number of times I join loving and loved together when naming how I practiced love is testament to love's inherent mutuality.

Still

Of course, one way to be still and silent that we may all call to mind is meditation. In one session, my spiritual director asked, "Do you meditate?" My first response was, "No." Because I don't tend to sit cross-legged on the floor with a candle and a mantra such as the "Jesus prayer."[15] And then I thought further. Wait, yes I do practice meditation. I sit. After breakfast and cleaning teeth and putting on my shoes and I am ready to leave, I often have five, ten, even 20 minutes before it is time to leave the house. Then, I return to my breakfast chair—the inside or the outside one—and I sit. I breathe. Sometimes listening intentionally to the birds or the breeze, the cars or the rain. Sometimes I do pray a "mantra", "Be still and know that I am God." Sometimes I call to mind the folk with whom I will meet that day, or for whom I am committed to praying, or for whom I know there are current joys or challenges. Farley talks about such prayer as presence, with each other and with God.[16]

And Mondays, my non-negotiable full day off, are intentionally still, silent days I spend in solitude. I stay at my Wee Hermitage. Perhaps I attend to the hermitage with laundry or dishes. Perhaps I engage in a jigsaw puzzle or cross stitch, in coloring or journaling or reading. These tasks for me have the element of meditation that is to pause, be still, and pay attention. Many of these are playful practices. As Edgar observes, to play leads one to a deepened capacity for prayer; play develops our inner life, and is about imagining what *could be*, as with prayer, fostering empathy, which *is*

---

15. Farley notes some expectations many have inherited, on which we may trip up as we attempt to find helpful meditation or contemplative practices: *Beguiled by Beauty*, 83, 97, 139.

16. Farley, *Beguiled by Beauty*, 114.

imagination.[17] Play is not about "games", but rather "an attitude to God and to the life God gives."[18]

Tricia Hersey encourages the kind of restful pause we can take between meetings, between jobs, even when finances mean we cannot yet escape the hustle: Or,

> Dragging my tired body out onto the streets to walk to the bus stop on my way to an underpaid forty-plus-hours-a-week job. I then would just stare out the window of the moving train, gaining a moment of peace and calm. I connected with the sky, watched the movement of the trees, possibly spotting a favorite bird. Those moments intensely settled my spirit. While I was living these moments, I just knew I felt better. The opportunity to breathe deeply while resting my eyes became a lifeline. I know now that these were moments of rest. I was able to pull back my mind from the grind and settle into my pure existence to just be and to reclaim my body as my own.[19]

I am learning that for one with ME/CFS, rest between things is a key to pacing, the core management strategy for the illness. To give the body a break from standing or sitting up by sitting with feet elevated if not actually lying down, allows us to rest.[20] I can feel the pressure release when I can let my head fall back onto the wingback armchair in my lounge room or office: five minutes can restore enough energy for another half an hour upright.

I have also found myself naming my practice of stillness not only as rest, afternoon naps, or a moment of pause on the patio. I find stillness in adopting a gentle pace through the day, choosing to be unhurried, choosing to decline panic's invitation. I find stillness in the movement of conversation, or swimming, or even a walk. Stillness, calm, presence, peace. It is posture through movement as much as it is ceasing movement by sitting still or lying down.

---

17. Edgar, *God Who Plays*, 12, 13, 9.
18. Edgar, *God Who Plays*, 17.
19. Hersey, *Rest is Resistance*, 31.
20. As I heard explained by Dr Brayden Yellman of the Bateman Horne Center, in relation to Orthostatic Intolerance, a feature of ME/CFS: https://www.youtube.com/watch?v=cGQFGgb_PtA; see also https://batemanhornecenter.org/wp-content/uploads/2023/09/Orthostatic-Intolerance-Education-Handout.pdf

Moving

"The body is an essential dimension of our spiritual life . . . it houses the Beloved."[21] I consider myself to be moving sometimes when I am lying down—active attentive breathing, meditating, paying attention to the Divine, for example. And, most obviously, movement is about physical activity or exercise. I like to walk. For a time, I swam. In my present season, the physical movement part of my practice is often lacking. This is a challenge for one with ME/Chronic Fatigue Syndrome, for the balance is intricate. Movement can help, but too much will immobilize me for days. That is why I find immersion in water helpful. I still grieve the loss of my swim-spa pool from former years, something I had to give up with my sudden move back to my home town without having a long-term residence lined up, to which I could relocate the pool. Rebuilding my life, I have been gentle and kind with myself, trying different options for warm water. I have taken classes with exercise physiologists, a membership at a local gym, gentle aquarobics classes a five-minute drive from home, hydrotherapy at a rehab center with mum. I have found that I have enough capacity for short walks again, and have visited the beach or incorporated walks down the shop- and café-lined street on which my church is located into days I work from there. The main challenge is to find some sort of rhythm. But commitment to discipline, if it is to be life-giving, must include compassion and gratitude for the moments we do well, and understanding that a new day begins tomorrow with another opportunity to practice the discipline again.

This discipline of movement is also about, for me, movement of thought, the practice of learning, stretching my mind, or my muscles of creativity. Movement may be progress with a project or idea, or through discernment and decision making, or forgiveness and healing. For my overall wellbeing, I need to move each day, all of me, body, spirit, mind.

Listening

The postures dovetail into each other, and so movement dovetails into listening, both ways in which I seek to be always learning. Remember Evers-Hood's observation that David has the capacity for lament, for presence in the sorrow, because David *listens*?[22] I have made a commitment to listen to a

---

21. Farley, *Beguiled by Beauty*, 142.
22. Evers-Hood, *Irrational David*, 109.

wide range of voices, of stories. To look out each day for the voices to which I pay attention. What am I learning? What am I hearing to help me grow? Who am I holding in their story, for their healing and wellbeing? And how am I listening to myself? Living with chronic illness, I have had to learn to listen well to my self, for how I am travelling, for what I need when I am not travelling so well. Again, Evers-Hood highlights the wisdom to be gleaned from the story of David: "It is only because David listens to Saul that he is sensitive to his moods and knows when and what music to play," to bring him comfort and ease.[23] To listen in the Hebrew Bible is to hear *and act* in response to what you've heard.

Perhaps "if we recover our ability to . . . vocalize our lament [for example], we will be strong enough to hear the voices of those crying out in pain;" and even when those voices name *us* as the cause of their pain.[24] It is quite some discipline to listen to the voices many dismiss. I deeply appreciate being in a community and a movement, the Uniting Church in Australia, committed to listening to the marginalized, and to our First Nations kin in particular.

There is another voice we seldom heed, even within much of the religious tradition. As an aside, I wonder if that goes hand in hand with our dismissal of cultures more attuned to Spirit, such as First Nations peoples in these lands now called Australia? Although we live in a culture in "the West" of "spiritual but not religious," we may yet observe that spirituality, and in particular, a contemplative way of being, is in our time largely ignored. So that there is much like a tide within and beyond the church influencing us to listen to the rational, to our selfish greed, to "success."[25] Although I had heard it for a long time, I resisted *listening* to the call of a contemplative way of being. Gradually, however, I have nurtured attentiveness and courage, so that I am now more than ever before embracing the voices of intuition, emotion, mystery; and voices long silenced and ignored by the Western culture in which I am located, women, Jewish, Blak/Black,[26] First Nations, poets. I am at last embracing a contemplative way of play, story, presence.

23. Evers-Hood, *Irrational David*, 209: David also "listens when Shimei . . . curses him," and later when he begs forgiveness.

24. Evers-Hood, *Irrational David*, 210.

25. Zimmer, *Leadership and Listening*, 138, 146.

26. This is how I understand many First Nations Peoples in Australia to refer to themselves: see Kate L. Munro, "Why 'Blak' not Black? Artist Destiny Deacon and the origins of this word". Produced by NITV/SBS. 29 June 2020 / 28 November 2022. https://www.sbs.com.au/nitv/article/

A CONTEMPLATIVE WAY OF BEING

Voiced

How do I use my voice? Do I speak with kindness, compassion, guided by wisdom? Do I shut up when it is time for someone else to be heard? Have I told a good story, told the Sacred story faithfully, shown someone their story has been heard? And how do I speak to myself?

In many ways, the story of finding and nurturing my voice is told through and between the lines of this book. Finding a playful voice, a courageous, risk-taking voice that spoke possibilities to and with a church community longing to grow from within through and beyond their edges, with Black Wood Jazz. With The Esther Project, starting to claim an alternative way of forming community, of gathering for worship, for myself and fellow creatives—paradoxically, perhaps, finding my own voice in resistance to the overly word-soaked ways to which our Protestant tradition had become accustomed.

A most profound way of finding my voice was identifying the storyteller within. From childhood, as I learned to read by recognizing on the page the words of the stories I heard my parents read to me, crafting and telling and playing stories out. The Year 7 teacher who gave me the Writers' Folder, the first time I had the writer so intentionally named for me. Again, finding my voice with resistance, rejecting English as a subject for my final year at school. I had found it too unsettling to write for a teacher and not be understood through Year 11. Literature remained with me through other subjects, however: I used Dickens and Barret Browning in a History assignment on the English Industrial Revolution. I went on to embrace French literature and as I mentioned, the Language, Literature, and the Law topic in my first degree at Uni. My voice. An alternative path, a slantwise approach.

The storyteller, the preacher, the pastor, prophet, priest, uses her voice by first listening. Mostly, actually, I reflect back what I hear and notice as I pay attention. I speak in a way that will invite those who hear to hear not only my story, but more importantly, their story and our story together. On my better days, I use my voice so as to empower the voices of others.

---

why-blak-not-black-artist-destiny-deacon-and-the-origins-of-this-word/7gv3mykzv. In *Rest is Resistance,* Tricia Hersey uses "Black"—women, people, Ancestors.

Part Three: Be

In creation

I have shared with you already the importance for me of being in creation and how I enact this practice. Sometimes the way I am still is also the way I have been attentive in creation; sometimes movement was practiced as I practiced presence with creation. Some days it will be paying attention with gratitude to the garden through the office window, the sun through the car window. Some days it will be a 30-minute walk on the beach, feet in water and sand through toes; or it might be an afternoon at the zoo. Some days it will be listening to the birds without stepping outside at all. Many days, it is at least garden bathing as I sit on the patio with breakfast, coffee, or lunch. The point is to remember, each day, to pay attention, with gratitude, to creation, the life around us, created, as we are, and named by Holy One as "good".

On the healing nature of green

after reading Phosphorescence, by Julia Baird

1. "I see trees of green"

as I read her reflections
on light in the dark,
on the healing to be found
in nature;
the experts she cites,
whose research uncovered
healing for folk who see green
every day;
I look

to my right where my pot plants
bask in the morning sun
through curtains I leave open
for them, in case I sleep in;
the next window along frames
the bush of magenta and gold roses,
no longer adorning branches of rich
dark green leaves;
looking ahead past kitchen,

over dining table and chairs,
or further left across the sofa
strewn with cushions and cross stitch
canvas and threads—

bushes, trees, leaves of every
shade of green are all
I can see;

later, when the sun moves around
I will take her book to the papasan
chair on the porch, my turn
to bask in sun light and green,
accompanied by the bees who love
the red flowery branches screening
my outside nook.

All that green, I see;
all the green they say
will heal,
and yet—

and yet, I am still

2. Well enough.
Remember the words of another,
writing to you, I speak gently
to myself;
the words of wonder as you fight
to live life as fully as you can,
as you achieve, and create,
though you pay some heavy price?

Remember the words used
to describe your quiet,
lonely hero's journey through each long day—
remember?

And I look again to my pot plants,
the bushes and trees, all that

> green and I gush gratitude: for what
> part they must play in carrying
> this lonely heroine through her days,
> I can but wonder,
> in awe.[27]

Loving, and loved

Rachel Held Evans reminds us in her final book that the "desire to be loved and to belong is . . . inherent to us all. It helps make us human."[28] She cites Brené Brown, whose writing also articulates for me things I know to be true: "We are biologically, cognitively, physically, and spiritually wired to love, to be loved, and to belong."[29] Mutuality.

Even knowing this to be true, it still can feel confronting as I consider each day how and who I "loved". To encourage myself to name a kindness, an act of generosity or care, as an act of love, especially for an acquaintance or stranger, seems bold. And yet, this is the command. This is the story: who is my neighbor? The one to whom I show love. As Jesus taught in Luke 10:25–37, for example.

And how I have been loved, received love? Again I have pushed through reluctance many times to name graciousness in response to my withdrawal from a commitment as *love* I have received. Because it is. Love as Jesus taught us.

Most often, the delight of the season in which I write this chapter, I bracket the two, loving and loved, and simply write the names of my niece and nephews; my sisters, mum, brothers-in-law: "family". For I am back in physical proximity to the family of my birth after seven years away, and I receive that as a welcome gift from an unexpected turn of events.

Postures that hold

In the years of rebuilding after the sudden end to a placement, I finally embedded the practice of daily reflection on these seven behaviors. This was a

---

27. Sarah Agnew, "On the healing nature of green", *Whisper on My Palm*, 24.

28. Rachel Held Evans, with Jeff Chu. *Wholehearted Faith*. New York, NY: HarperCollins, 2021, 74.

29. Brené Brown. *Daring Greatly: How the Courage to Be Vulnerable Transforms the Way We Live, Love, Parent, and Lead*. New York, NY: Penguin Random House, 2015, 145.

practice that helped hold the pieces of my broken self. There wasn't much of that rhythm I described earlier, during this season. For a while, every day was a rest day, in my incapacitated, burnt out, state.

Gradually, I took on various jobs, or fulfilled previously-made commitments like writing liturgy, or leading a three-day retreat in NSW. More writing, some editing, and eventually, some preaching and another retreat or two. I also took the opportunity to work on this writing project—this is a book I have been writing and rewriting for 15 years, if you believe it! I sat on the porch on warm Autumn days; took my notebook to the beach or a café, and wrote the fourth or fifth iteration of a book that looks barely like the one I began so long ago.

When I was invited to teach, and explore some other editing and writing work, I asked if I could use the spare office at my family church. This congregation had welcomed me back with such a warm and gentle embrace, and they let me use the office for no charge. Over Advent and Christmas, I offered some creative input to our worship gatherings, for no charge. They and I have been in a mutually encouraging relationship for the better part of 30 years, even across great distance. I tried to keep a rhythm of sorts with the office; certain days were good for company, others for quiet. Teaching built some rhythm with the set times for turning up to class. Even so, this season was still very much one day at a time. So, finishing the day with a reflection on the seven practices, committing myself to living, even in that unexpected unusual season, according to those postures I trust align me with the Holy was an exercise in discipline I had never enacted with such sustained commitment before.

Eighteen months on, talking with my spiritual director, I expressed ongoing dissatisfaction with my morning habits. I wake, push snooze on the alarm, then continue to resist waking up by checking the socials, emails, playing games. Not an attentive way to enter the day. Could I, I wondered, take my seven postures and shape a new morning practice? Gentle. Invitational. More rhythm than routine. Yes, I can. I determined to learn from my experience with the close of day practice, which took a number of years to settle and become something I miss if I do not do it. I will—and one says these things with a spiritual director knowing she will hold you accountable to your commitment—I will start, I will play with some ideas, and I will be kind to myself when I do well for a day and then not so well for three. It will take time. I suspect I will look for a noon / lunch time practice in time too, but I very deliberately put that aside for now. I leave that as a gift to play with in another season. Always learning. Always growing. One change at a time. The practice of stillness through my days—my playful meditation—is showing its effect in this patience. In past seasons I have tended to want to do all the things, implement all my ideas, all at once. I quite like this me I am rebuilding in the aftermath of a traumatic season. I am building a smaller, quieter life. I am claiming a new facet of my identity as a contemplative, and I do like it.

The opportunity to play with being freelance did, as I mentioned, offer more fluidity to my weeks, which meant I could work when I had energy, and rest when I needed. It was a long time feeling broken, and the short-term jobs were helpful with their gentler kind of commitment. And I got to play with, experiment with, some different expressions of those eclectic gifts I have shown you. Working as a writer was a lovely moment I noticed with gratitude. Not overly well paid, but my main source of income for a short while, it was some kind of realization of an old, old dream. A working writer. Editing was a job I had happily let go some years before, but picking it up again, I remembered what I liked about it, the playing with language. One job also had me working with Biblical Hebrew again, after many years.

The invitation to teach brought the biblical languages more fully back onto my plate. Studying the Bachelor when in formation for ordination, my lecturers identified an affinity for languages and encouraged me to take all three available levels of both New Testament Greek and Biblical Hebrew. A minister only *needs* one semester or level of one of these languages. Straight out of the Bachelor, I taught Biblical Hebrew, with no other better qualified people available. In recent years, I had become one of three of our NBS seminar who fairly often provide new translations for performance as we explore together various biblical compositions. I had thought I didn't want to end up teaching the languages, but the invitation came in this season to teach Greek and the next year, Hebrew; a rhythm to which I could commit for years to come, it seemed. I am one of a small number in the Uniting Church in Australia who can teach both biblical languages on the syllabus of our theological colleges. I decided to accept the invitation, not only because it was paid work and I needed it (sometimes I can be practical); also, because the college needed what I could offer. I can do this, and perhaps a change in direction will yield surprise and delight, I wondered. Perhaps I can do more work with translations, write and publish in that area. Perhaps I can enthuse others and equip them to find meaning and communicate effectively in English for our time and contexts. A playful posture, an open posture, paying attention and being willing to try and for it *not* to work out. And it started off well, and I enjoyed bringing the perspective of a performer to the teaching of languages. Then my health faltered again, and life needed to become even smaller.

As I rebuild my life in this season, I am letting go of the hustle of the freelancer, trusting that invitations will come my way and I may say yes or no as gladly, depending on what my capacity is at any given moment. It's Brown's courage, compassion, and connection again. I do not fear being overlooked, the invitations not coming, because I trust the relationships I have built and my presence within a community, and I trust that I am enough. Present with myself, with Holy One, with community, I know myself to belong and to be enough. Still before I move, silent before I speak, connected to creation and Creator, loving as I am loved. Postures that hold me, well.

~

Pause

Have you followed particular "rules", perhaps of monastic communities, or rhythms, or disciplines? How have they nurtured your wellbeing?

If you haven't thus far, I wonder if you feel intrigued enough to explore further?

Benedictine and Jesuit rules may be places to start.

Perhaps the stories of Hildegard of Bingen or Julian of Norwich may invite you into a contemplative way of being.

~

Place: The Wee Hermitage

Speaking of being held, this season of rebuilding a life more contemplative has featured a new home. I lived for four years in a large manse, which I delighted in making my home. That was a season of plenty, financially, in a full-time placement after three years as a struggling PhD student. I took my time to choose furnishings, and did *try* not to fill the space simply because it was there.

Part Three: Be

However, as I had some space, I did experiment with some different kinds of seating to hold my aching, fatigued body. Wing back armchairs, lounges, a therapy pod (which is like a beanbag, but filled with bits of memory foam). I also kept many craft and worship supplies, and filled the bookshelves both at home and in my office at the church.

This new place is smaller by far. The large square dining table for eight I had long loved, and which my sister squeezed into her place for me while I was in Scotland, had to go. The sofa-bed bought with 40th birthday gift vouchers, sold. Cupboards, an exercise machine, books, and the piano from our childhood home, all gone. Even so, I still had too much to squeeze into the new place. Once moved in, there was that therapy pod to part with, an armchair to house in my new office whenever I got a job, and more books to put on a garage sale.

Some months in, starting to really embrace this space in its smallness, I emptied boxes of English Literature papers from 20 years ago, and journals even older than that. When I buy new clothes now, I try to let go of the ones I no longer wear. I taught myself to darn socks rather than replace them, and I used up all the old Christmas paper, and then the fabric gift bags my sister started making, rather than buying more paper for the season.

Life in the Wee Hermitage is a small, content life. I still furnish on a principle of joy—and what gives me joy now is simplicity. From my retreat up the hill from the city I built a rhythm of time in community with time alone. I am on the edges of the broad neighborhood of suburbs that I consider "home", in which my immediate family still live, and I am deeply grateful for a season of physical proximity with them again. I am part of their everyday life, Aunt Sarah in the village raising the next generation, sisterly company for walks and concerts and movies, daughter for long chats over coffee or champagne. Gently, though, for they have come to understand my solitude, my hermit-like life as precious in support of my wellbeing. More days than not, now, I stay at the Hermitage, still, silent, in solitude—nurturing that inner peace from which I can offer hospitable presence for others.

Rebuilding my life as a contemplative is shaping my home, and my wee hermitage is supporting my desire to become a contemplative in my posture and way of being.

∽

A way to play, to tell, to be

The gift of the unwelcome circumstance of chronic illness has been that it offered me a path into a more contemplative way of being that I had long pondered, but somehow had not managed to enact. I am sure it is not only the illness and its enforcing of stillness and solitude. Of course, I have grown and learnt and experienced life some more each year. I have heard and I have told stories to challenge and inspire. I have developed a capacity to listen to myself, to my being as it is yearning to become. I listen for what I need for wellbeing, for healing, for wholeness, and I have courage born of experience to do it, without caring what anyone thinks as I do. For the guiding principle is who, and how, do I want to be, contemplative creative woman of Holy One? And there's integrity in that; or authenticity at least, I hope. Further, I do not ask that question for myself alone. For I have come to know deep in my being that we (created life) are whole only with each other.

Invitation to reflect

Is presence a posture you take in your various roles in life?

What gift/s does, or might, presence offer you and your community?

What might be the cause of any reluctance you feel to adopting a posture of presence more often?

Is there another posture you take, which my reflections on presence brings to mind for you?

Do you have questions of my story or the ideas I have explored; of yourself and your story?

How will you explore your questions with curiosity? Journal, art, meditation, talking with others?

Postlude

True belonging is the spiritual practice of believing and belonging to yourself so deeply that you can share your most authentic self with the world and find sacredness in both being a part of something and standing alone in the wilderness. True belonging doesn't require you to change who you are; it requires you to be who you are.

Brené Brown, *Dare to Lead*

Not to lead, but to accompany each other

To play.

To imagine.

To so embrace my vulnerability as to open myself to creativity, innovation, and empathy.

To tell.

To facilitate.

To be storied, storying, re-storying, for the nurture of wellbeing, community, connection.

To be.

To be present.

To pay attention from a posture of contemplation finding identity and belonging with Holy One.

POSTLUDE

As with the vocation of storyteller-poet-minister, dynamic interplay of three facets of calling and identity, play, story, and presence weave together with vitality.

I did not set out to be a leader, and as I now understand, leaders are made by followers anyway, not themselves. I am learning that I am a leader when and as others name me as such by choosing to follow, asking me to accompany them. I am interested in how I have and continue to respond, as people choose to follow me, reading, listening, seeking my presence. And I am interested in a ministry of presence, in accompanying each other, in mutuality. We are fully human only together, and what's more, only with all creation.

Mutuality

MY STORY HAS WOVEN a thread of "mutuality" throughout. As I draw this story to a close with the depiction of my contemplative way of being, or rule for living, I want to revisit this central motif of my story and my life. This contemplative way of living and leading is a practice of radical presence, of *being with*.

with

we need more "with"—
sitting beside and listening,
standing beside and supporting,
opening arms in welcome:
we need more "with".

we need longer tables
and more plates;
broader dance floors—
more dancing.
we need more "with".

and we need more love:
eyes open to see,
blinking with our weeping;
reaching out and holding hands:
we need more love.

> we need kinder hearts
> and broader smiles,
> open doors,
> lower fences.
> we need more love.
>
> we need
> more compassion:
> more us,
> more "thank you";
> more we,
> more "welcome";
> more together,
> more "you matter";
> more we differ
> and that's brilliant;
> more you differ
> and that's a gift;
> more together,
> more "you matter";
> more us,
> more "with",
> more love,
> more compassion.
> we need
> more
> compassion.[1]

Mutuality was at the core of my doctoral exploration of the New Testament letter to Rome, not to mention the method I developed for such explorations.

> *Mutuality* has a quality of mutual obligation born of mutual need; of other-regard that seeks the good of the other first, *and also* good of self. For people of faith, "God is the basis of mutual relation."[2] This goal of good for the other is not entirely selfless, however. The give and take of relationships of true mutuality *is* intrinsically beneficial to both parties to the relationship. Mutuality is paradoxical:

---

1. Agnew, "with". *Whisper on My Palm*, 18.
2. Ehrensperger, Kathy. *That We May Be Mutually Encouraged*. New York: T. & T. Clark (2004), 118.

its outcome of good for the self is a consequence of the objective of seeking good for the other.[3]

As I had noted in my honors thesis, mutuality is "a deep honoring of the dignity and worth of the other as bound up in my own dignity and worth; and I cannot honor one if I do not honor the other."[4]

> In his letter to the Romans, Paul seeks to encourage mutuality as a feature of the Christ-following communities in Rome.[5] Their relationships are to be those of mutual encouragement, accommodating one another, as Christ accommodates God's beloved, welcoming, loving, embracing, and thereby inhabiting one another's space. But they are to maintain their own identity, subjects apart, Jew *and* Gentile: not assimilate one group's identity into another's. Difference is not to be overcome, but is rather a "presupposition for real unity."[6] . . . Mutuality needs both the individual and the communal, distinctness and difference along with unity and togetherness. . . . Paul's vision of Christian community is one that celebrates difference, indeed welcomes it, for the opportunity it provides for mutual embrace of one another.[7]

In a later season, I reflected on Romans 12 with my congregation, and Paul's explicit invitation in this latter part of the letter into "mutual embrace."

> Paul's letter to Rome reminds us of the reconciling love of God in which we participate, when we choose this Way of Life. When we choose to accept the restoration into the fulness of life offered in God through Christ, Paul tells us, we are also choosing to be transformed into a reconciling way of being—reconciling one to another.
>
> Of course, it's not as simple in the living as it is to say, as [we know] from the different seasons that bring intense change to relationships of mutual belonging and embrace. Because an embrace is both comforting and challenging, if we're honest.

---

3. Agnew, *Embodied Performance*, 26.
4. Agnew, "Mutuality of Esther and Mordecai", 72.
5. Following such scholars as Ehrensperger, *Paul and the Dynamics of Power*, 55; Gaventa, "The Cosmic Power of Sin in Paul's Letter to the Romans: Towards a Widescreen Edition." *Interpretation* 58 (2004), 236; and Oestreich, *Performance Criticism of the Pauline Letters*, 174–75.
6. Ehrensperger, *Mutually Encouraged*, 199.
7. Agnew, *Embodied Performance*, 27–28.

Part Three: Be

I heard in the code of ethics session recently the notion of our congregations holding the potential for intimacy in relationship—not sexual intimacy, to which "intimate" has been limited somewhat in its use. But the kind of intimacy that *is* embrace—there's a Welsh word I came across this week—*Cwtch*- kudj. The Facebook post said this: "more than a cuddle or a hug, when you give someone a *cwtch*, you figuratively give them a 'safe place.'"

But to open yourself to give and to receive such an embrace, to *be* safe, paradoxically, you must make yourself vulnerable. Vulnerable to the unsettling that comes when our differences feel uncomfortable up close together—and then it can be hard to stay close.... When we say we are a community of mutual embrace, it is to say we choose to nurture trust, intimacy, presence—we choose to offer safety in which we can continue to be vulnerable in order to hold each other close, in belonging, in wholeness together.[8]

Learning to accompany and live well

I TELL MY STORY for us, as an act of mutual embrace. And what I have sought to tell you here are stories through which I learned. Learned I am one who is willing to play. To explore new territory, to make mistakes and find the magic there.[9] Learned I am a storyteller. Happy to be before an audience, or presiding in a gathered community (when most people find that terrifying, apparently). I am one who holds, reflects on deeply, learns, and tells the Sacred Story of my faith tradition. I compose and tell stories in many formats; I write poetry and liturgy; I am prophet, priest, and I am pastor. I hold the stories of others, curious, delighting, and unafraid of the stories of suffering and shadows. Learned I am, as I long suspected, a contemplative. Paying attention to the Sacred, turning towards Them, aligning myself with Holy One. I am growing in discipline, developing practices, living a rhythm of stillness and solitude, community and connection, knowing that rather than "lead" you, I would prefer to accompany you, in mutual encouragement on a Way of Love.

My rule, my practice, this contemplative way of being looks in practice like this.

---

8. Agnew, Sarah. "Who we say we are. Mutually Embracing." sarahagnew.com.au/mutually-embracing/ 13 September 2023.

9. Dench, *Shakespeare*, 198.

POSTLUDE

The week begins with a Hermitage Day. Silent. Still. Solitude. What some may call a Sabbath.

I spend two days in the church building, present with and for the congregation. I then spend three days based at the Hermitage, more stillness, with rest for a day, play for half a day, taking my nephew to a music program, then gently attending to congregation and college folk and tasks over the next day and a half. I spend a day present with the congregation, the morning in the building, the afternoon more often than not replenishing the energy that holding the gathered congregation requires with a Sacred Sunday Snooze.

Each day, I aim to rise and move to the couch to listen to stories from the world around me. I sit, still, and I pray. Then I eat breakfast on the patio, or in the tub chair looking out to the garden.

During the day I am aware I want to be still, to move and learn, to listen more than I speak; I seek to be attentively in creation, to look with love and be open to receive the gift of love when it is offered to me. These are not tasks to tick off a list, not jobs "to do". No, this is about postures and practices, about the ways I find I can be my authentic self, whose identity is found in the Divine.

At the close of the day, I take note of the stillness and the movement, the ways I listened and used my voice. I remember how I was present with creation, how I gave and received love.

On Sunday evenings, I also reflect on how this week I played, I entered story, I was present, and where I encountered Holy One.

This is a practice of presence, of paying attention. It is a contemplative way of being. There are chords, some strict, some with more incidentals. There is commitment to the chords, the structure, the postures and practices that hold me in my living. This is life lived from my Wee Hermitage, where I nurture inner peace that enables me to connect with community—always learning how to live, to lead (accompany), and *be*, well.

Play. Tell. Be.
A Rule of Sacred Presence.

At the close of each day, I reflect on my chosen practices:

Stillness
Movement
Listening
Voiced
In creation
Loving
Loved

Each Sunday evening, I reflect on my chosen postures:

Play.
Tell.
Be.
Aligned with Holy One.

Reflect

I wonder, what practices do you choose to shape a life lived well?

What postures will or already do enable you to lead and live, well?

Appendix
Wellbeing resources

Myalgic Encephalomyelitis / Chronic Fatigue Syndrome

https://batemanhornecenter.org

https://www.cdc.gov/me-cfs/toolkit/index.html

https://mecfssa.org.au

https://www.nhs.uk/conditions/chronic-fatigue-syndrome-cfs/

https://www.youtube.com/watch?v=cGQFGgb_PtA

Network Spinal Chiropractic

https://www.vitalwisdom.com.au

https://lifewise.net.au/network-care-adelaide/?doing_wp_cron=174606 5456.5426371097564697265625

EFT/Tapping (Emotional Freedom Techniques)

https://lighthouseeft.com.au/resources/science-of-tapping/

https://eftuniverse.com/research-studies/

Bibliography

Adegbite, Shola. "The Story Must Go On: Biblical Storytelling as Unfinished Business", NBSI Scholars Seminar, 30 July 2024.
Agnew, Sarah. *Embodied Performance. Mutuality, Embrace, and the Letter to Rome.* Eugene, OR: Pickwick, 2020.
———. "Of the Instant Goodbyes." *From the Mist*, 25. Eugene, OR: Resource, 2025.
———. "The Mutuality of Esther and Mordecai: Narrative Analysis and Embodied Performance Preparation of Esther 4". Flinders University, 2013.
———. *On Wisdom's Wings.* Adelaide: Ginninderra Press, 2013.
———. *Pray the Story.* Canberra: Self-published, 2019.
———. "A Presence Assumed." For *Act2 Theological Culture Papers,* Produced by Uniting Church in Australia Assembly, 11 Oct 2023. https://act2uca.com/theological-culture/a-presence-assumed/
———. "On the Healing Nature of Green." *Whisper on My Palm*, 24. Eugene, OR: Resource, 2022.
———. "With." *Whisper on My Palm*, 18. Eugene, OR: Resource, 2022.
———. "Who We Say We Are. Mutually Embracing." sarahagnew.com.au/mutually-embracing/ 13 September 2023.
Agnew, Sarah. Jason Chesnut (dir.), "03. Romans 1 Digital Storytelling", 2017. Produced by Jason Chesnut, ANKOSFilms. sarahagnew.com.au/Embodied-Performance.
American Psychiatric Association. *Diagnostic and Statistical Manual of Mental Disorders: DSM-IV.* Washington, D.C.: American Psychiatric Association, 1994.
Aquilina, Jude, John Pfitzner, and Russell Talbot (Eds). *Season of a New Heart.* Adelaide: Effective Living Centre, 2010.
Assembly of the Uniting Church in Australia: https://uniting.church
Baird, Julia. *Phosphorescence. On Awe, Wonder, and Things that Sustain You when the World Goes Dark.* Sydney: Fourth Estate, 2020.
Bargár, Pavol. *Embodied Existence. Our Common Life in God.* Eugene, OR: Cascade, 2023.
Bateman Horne Center. "Orthostatic Intolerance Education Handout." https://batemanhornecenter.org/wp-content/uploads/2023/09/Orthostatic-Intolerance-Education-Handout.pdf Accessed 2 June 2025.
Bechtel, Carol M. *Esther.* Interpretation. Louisville, KY: John Knox, 2002.
Bell, Rob. "Nooma 011: Rhythm—Rob Bell. Produced by Zondervan. YouTube, Aug 29, 2012. https://www.youtube.com/watch?v=1FNH0Yl8a78.
Bos, Rob and Geoff Thompson (Eds), *Theology for Pilgrims. Selected Theological Documents of the Uniting Church in Australia,* Sydney: The Assembly of the Uniting Church in Australia, 2008.
Brown, Brené. *Dare to Lead. Brave Work. Tough Conversations. Whole Hearts.* London, UK: Vermilion, 2018.

BIBLIOGRAPHY

———. *Daring Greatly: How the Courage to Be Vulnerable Transforms the Way We Live, Love, Parent, and Lead*. New York, NY: Penguin Random House, 2015.

———. *The Gifts of Imperfection*. Center City: Hazelden, 2010.

Butler Bass, Diana. *Christianity for the Rest of Us: How the Neighborhood Church Is Transforming the Faith*. New York, NY: HarperCollins, 2009.

Costas, Orlando E. "The Subversiveness of Faith: Esther as a Paradigm for a Liberating Theology," *Ecumenical Review* 40, no. 1 (1988), 66–78.

Crossan, John Dominic. *The Greatest Prayer*. New York, NY: HarperCollins, 2010.

Day, Linda M. *Abingdon Old Testament Commentaries: Esther*. Nashville: Abingdon, 2005.

Dench, Judi with Brendan O'Hea. *Shakespeare. The Man Who Pays the Rent*. Dublin: Penguin Random House, 2023.

Edgar, Brian. *The God Who Plays. A Playful Approach to Theology and Spirituality*. Eugene, OR: Cascade, 2017.

Ehrensperger, Kathy. *Paul and the Dynamics of Power: Communication and Interaction in the Early Christ-Movement*. Library of New Testament Studies. Edited by Mark Goodacre. London, UK: T. & T. Clark, 2007.

———. *That We May Be Mutually Encouraged*. New York, NY: T. & T. Clark, 2004.

Evans, Rachel Held, with Jeff Chu. *Wholehearted Faith*. New York, NY: HarperCollins 2021.

Evers-Hood, Ken. *The Irrational David: The Power of Poetic Leadership*. Eugene, OR: Wipf and Stock, 2019.

Farley, Wendy. *Beguiled by Beauty. Cultivating a Life of Contemplation and Compassion*. Louisville, KY: Westminster John Knox, 2020.

Gaventa, Beverly Roberts. "The Cosmic Power of Sin in Paul's Letter to the Romans: Towards a Widescreen Edition." *Interpretation* 58 (2004) 229–40.

Gooder, Paula. *Phoebe. A Story*, London: Hodder & Stoughton, 2018.

Gordis, Robert. "Studies in the Esther Narrative," *Journal of Biblical Literature* 95.1 (1976) 43–58.

Goto, Courtney T. *The Grace of Playing. Pedagogies for Leaning into God's New Creation*. Eugene, OR: Pickwick, 2016,

Hersey, Tricia. *Rest is Resistance*. London: Aster, 2022.

Kelsey, David H. *Eccentric Existence. A Theological Anthropology*. 2 Volumes. Louisville: Westminster John Knox, 2009.

Levenson, Jon D. *Esther*, Old Testament Library. London: SCM Ltd, 1997.

Lings, George. "Looking in the Mirror: What Makes a Pioneer?" in *Pioneers 4 Life. Explorations in Theology and Wisdom for Pioneering Leaders*, edited by Dave Male. Abingdon, 30–47. UK: Bible Reading Fellowship, 2011.

Male, Dave. "The Icebergs of Expectation: Personal Issues Pioneers Face", in *Pioneers 4 Life. Explorations in Theology and Wisdom for Pioneering Leaders*, edited by Dave Male, 67–75. Abingdon, UK: Bible Reading Fellowship, 2011.

Martin, Philip. *The Zen Path through Depression*. United Kingdom: HarperCollins, 1999.

McKenna, Megan. *Keepers of the Story. Oral Traditions in Religion*. New York, NY: Seabury, 2004.

Munro, Kate L. "Why 'Blak' not Black? Artist Destiny Deacon and the origins of this word". Produced by NITV/SBS, 29 June 2020 / 28 November 2022 https://www.sbs.com.au/nitv/article/why-blak-not-black-artist-destiny-deacon-and-the-origins-of-this-word/7gv3mykzv.

Nolasco, Rolf Jr. *The Contemplative Counselor. A Way of Being*. Minneapolis: Fortress, 2011.

BIBLIOGRAPHY

Oestreich, Bernhard. *Performance Criticism of the Pauline Letters.* Translated by Lindsay Elias and Brent Blum. Biblical Performance Criticism Series 14. Eugene, OR: Cascade, 2016.

Purnell, Douglas. *Being in Ministry. Honestly, Openly, and Deeply.* Eugene, OR: Wipf & Stock, 2010

Riddell, Mike, Mark Pierson, and Cathy Kirkpatrick. *Prodigal Project. Journey into the Emerging Church.* London: SPCK, 2000.

Song, Angeline. "Heartless Bimbo or Subversive Role Model?: A Narrative (Self) Critical Reading of the Character of Esther," *Dialog: A Journal of Theology* 49, no. 1 (2010), 56–69.

Sutch Pickard, Jan. *Out of Iona. Words from a Crossroads of the World.* Glasgow: Wild Goose, 2003.

Taylor, Daniel. *Creating a Spiritual Legacy: How to Share Your Stories, Values, and Wisdom.* Grand Rapids, MI: Baker Publishing Group, 2011.

Tenny, Tommy, with Mark Andrew Olsen, *Hadassah. One Night with the King.* Minneapolis, MN: Bethany House, 2004.

Uniting Church in Australia. *The Basis of Union.* Adelaide: MediaCom, 1977 & 1992 (Rev. ed).

White, Sidnie Ann. "Esther: A Feminine Model for Jewish Diaspora," in *Gender and Difference in Ancient Israel*, edited by Peggy L. Day, 161–77. Minneapolis: Fortress Press, 1989.

Yellman, Brayden. "Understanding Post-Exertional Malaise", Produced by The ME Action Network, April 24 2024. https://www.youtube.com/watch?v=cGQFGgb_PtA.

Yoder, Sue Pizor and Co.Lab.Inq. *Hear Us Out. Six Questions on Belonging and Belief.* Minneapolis: Fortress, 2023.

Zimmer, Donald E. *Leadership and Listening. Spiritual Foundations for Church Governance.* Herndon, VA: Alban Institute, 2011.

www.ingramcontent.com/pod-product-compliance
Lightning Source LLC
Chambersburg PA
CBHW060521090426
42735CB00011B/2321